Chester Preyar
508 Braden Dr.
Durham, NC 27713-9549

JOHN CALVIN
The Christian Life

**Edited by
John H. Leith**

WIPF & STOCK · Eugene, Oregon

Wipf and Stock Publishers
199 W 8th Ave, Suite 3
Eugene, OR 97401

The Christian Life
By Calvin, John
Copyright©1984 by Foundation for Reformed Theology
ISBN 13: 978-1-60608-743-5
Publication date 4/22/2009
Previously published by Harper & Row, 1984

Contents

Introduction

By John H. Leith

A THEOLOGY FOR PIETY

John Calvin, the Reformer of Geneva, wrote his greatest theological work as a summary of piety and of religion. Theology exists for the sake of piety. "Truth is in order to goodness; and the great touchstone of truth, its tendency to promote holiness."[1] Calvin was by commitment a practical, not a speculative, theologian. The purpose of theology is to edify, to transform human life and society, not so much to answer questions.

The negative aspect of this positive emphasis on edification is seen in Calvin's opposition to all idle curiosity and also to the attempt to pry into things that God has not revealed. True wisdom does not desire to know more than God has made known to us, but searches out how our lives can be edified, how we can grow in piety, and how our lives are given meaning by what God has revealed.

John Calvin (1509–1564) was himself a churchman who combined in one life the tasks of interpreting the Bible, of preaching, of pastoral care, and of leadership in the church generally. He wrote theology, not in the context of a university, but under the pressures of an active church community and amidst the conflicts and challenges of sixteenth-century Europe.

For twenty-five years, between 1536 and his death in 1564, Calvin was minister of the Word of God in Geneva, except for a brief time in exile from Geneva as pastor of the French church in Strasbourg from 1538–1541. After 1555 Calvin's influence was pervasive, and John Knox, a loyal supporter of Calvin, exclaimed that Geneva had become the most perfect school of Christ on earth since the days of the Apostles.

Calvin had also become an influential leader in the whole Protestant community. He was the pastor and adviser for countless Protestants in churches throughout Europe, especially in France, the Netherlands, England, and Scotland. His letters fill eleven volumes of his collected writings. His known sermons comprise one-third of his total writings, and including sermons known to be lost would equal one-half. The quantity of his letters and sermons indicates his practical concerns. Calvin's *Institutes of the Christian Religion* became the most influential and comprehensive Protestant statement of Christian faith.

When Calvin died in 1564, Pope Pius IV is said to have commented that Calvin's strength lay in the fact that he was never corrupted by money. His fellow ministers in Geneva noted that he subordinated his own self-interest to the work to which he was committed. His influence was founded on the agreement of his theology with his practice.

It is against this background of actual Christian life and responsibility for the community that Calvin wrote about piety. Piety is "that reverence joined with love of God which the knowledge of his benefits induces." The foundation of piety is an awareness that we owe everything to God, that we are nourished by his fatherly care, that he is the author of our every good, and that we should seek nothing beyond him. Piety is, therefore, an attitude or disposition toward God, evoked by an awareness of his benefits. It combines reverence with love. Piety, as the proper attitude toward God, is also a disposition toward creation as the work of God and toward the neighbor who bears the divine image. It is a matter of the heart which can be expressed in outward works but for which no outward works can become a substitute.

Piety is closely related in Calvin's thought to religion and faith. Religion is "faith so joined with an earnest fear of God, that this fear also embraces willing reverence, and carries with it such legitimate worship as is prescribed in the law." Religion is the embodiment of piety in ceremony and ritual. Faith is more specific than piety, relating primarily to redemption. It is "a firm and certain knowledge of God's benevolence toward us, founded upon the truth of the freely given promise in Christ, both revealed to our minds and sealed upon our hearts through the Holy Spirit."

Theology exists for faith, religion, and piety or, as Calvin liked to say, for edification. Calvin's work in Geneva was that of a preacher who was concerned that Christian faith should be embodied not simply in books, not simply in institutions, but primarily in Christian people living in the Christian community and in society.

THE PRACTICE OF THE FAITH

John Calvin, the theologian, gave unusual attention to the ordering of his theological thoughts. He expressed satisfaction that he had finally achieved, in the last edition of the *Institutes* in 1559, the proper arrangement of his thoughts about God's relationship with the Christian believer. Having discussed the doctrines of God, man, Jesus Christ, and salvation, Calvin brings together four sections of material which tell how faith expresses itself in the practice of the Christian life, in Christian freedom, in prayer, and in the conviction that all of this is rooted in the purposes of God and in the work of his Spirit. As pastor in Geneva, Calvin was concerned with the practical task of moving from theological affirmation to the concrete embodiment of that theology in the life of the individual and of the community. The material in this anthology should be read in light of this concern.

In the treatise on the Christian life Calvin intends to indicate, at least in broad outline, a pattern for the conduct of life. The practice of the Christian life, Calvin believed, is, above all, self-denial which has primary reference to the attitude and disposition of the human heart and cross-bearing, which is the outward expression of the inward disposition. For Calvin, the basic sin is unbelief, lack of trust and confidence in God the Father, but the primary expression of that sin is pride or self-centeredness. This self-centeredness is overcome by the practice of self-denial, which is both a dying unto self and also a becoming alive unto God and to one's fellow human beings. Cross-bearing has as its chief reference the ways in which the Christian relates to the challenges and crises of life. For Calvin, the cross is not a necessity but a voluntary task or suffering which is accepted out of faith and piety.

The Christian life is also holding in proper balance the present life and the life to come. Calvin was profoundly aware that this world of flesh and blood, bounded by nature and history, in which we live, is not the only world there is. He was convinced that it is not the most important world. There is another world at work within this world, another order of existence, that is enclosed neither by nature nor by history and which by God's grace moves to its fulfillment beyond nature and history. Hence, Calvin insists that Christian living involves meditation on the future life that puts the present life in proper perspective. In the chapter of the *Institutes* on the uses of the present life, Calvin exults in the goodness and wonder of God's creation and lays down certain principles to guide us in its use. "It is the hope of the life to come that gives meaning and purpose to the life in which we presently are." Calvin concludes with a marvelous statement on Christian vocation or calling, a very important theme for him, as for Martin Luther. He was convinced that the meaning of life is to be found in our embodiment, even in a broken and fragmentary way, of the purposes of God in our common life, in the home, and in our work. This conviction that we have been called by God, Calvin believed, transforms the humblest task into the most precious service of God.

Christian freedom was a clearly enunciated dimension of the Christian life as Calvin understood it, but it is likewise one that Calvinists have frequently forgotten. It is the practical, everyday embodiment of the doctrine of justification by grace through faith. Christians find their salvation and their security not in their own works or in their own achievements, but in the love and grace of God. This grace of God, which frees us from the obligation of having to merit God's favor, gives to life a spontaneity and freedom that can only express itself in joy. True Christian obedience finds its deepest motive not in the endeavor to win the favor of God or to buy his good pleasure, but as an expression of gratitude for the mercy which the Christian has already experienced.

Christian freedom also means that God alone is the Lord of the conscience and has left the conscience free from all the commandments and regulations of human beings. Luther and Calvin alike insisted that the Christian conscience can be bound not by society, not by powerful individuals, not by the church, but only by God. In the sphere of things indifferent, those areas of life that do not stand under a specific command of God, the Christian conscience is free. Yet Christians do not use their freedom to undermine the consciences of the weak. As the Apostle Paul declared, if eating meat that had been offered to idols should offend a weaker brother, then he would subordinate his freedom to eat the meat to his concern for his neighbor.

Calvin's discussion of prayer belongs with the great classic treatises such as those by the early Christian writers Tertullian, Gregory of Nyssa, and Augustine, as well as those of more recent times. In this chapter of the *Institutes* Calvin is concerned not so much with the theory of prayer, but with questions about how we ought to pray.

The prayers which are included in this anthology are taken from Calvin's catechism. The catechism was used as a manual of instruction for membership in the church, and the printing of the prayers at the conclusion of the catechism seems to indicate that Calvin was seeking to establish a pattern for the daily devotions of Christian people. In the *Institutes* he had suggested that each day Christians should set a pattern of prayer on awaking in the morning, before and after eating, on going to work, and on retiring at night.

Calvin is best known for his doctrine of predestination, which grew in part out of his own experience. He knew that if 100 people heard a sermon, perhaps only 10 or 20 would respond positively. The mystery of the human response to the gospel was also part of the more general mystery of human diversity. Some are born in the fellowship of the Christian family and some in a horrible social matrix. Some are born with good minds and healthy bodies, and others are not. For Calvin, the roots of this diversity in matters of faith as well as physical well-being are to be found in the hidden will of God, though at times Calvin seems to have an irrepressible desire to obscure the mystery by saying that the negative aspects of life are simply the expression of God's intention. Yet Calvin's emphasis lies on what God has made known of himself in Jesus Christ, and on the Christian experience of God's electing grace.

Calvin discusses election not at the beginning of his theology, not under the doctrine of God and God's providence, but at the end of his discussion of the Christian life immediately before the chapter on the resurrection of the body. This location of the doctrine in Calvin's theology suggests its role in the Christian life. When Christians look back on their lives and their experiences, they exclaim that God has done this in and through their lives, that all praise belongs to him.

Calvin believed that the doctrine of predestination is one of comfort. Our salvation does not depend upon our own achievements. It is not a matter of surface appearance or behavior. It is deeply rooted in the purposes of God, Creator of heaven and earth. God thought of us before we were, called us into being, gave to us our identity, our individuality, our name. God also has called us to be his holy people, and God has given us a work to do. Our daily lives in our homes, in our work, in our recreation, embody, at least in a broken and fragmentary way, the purposes of God. This deep conviction about God's intention and God's purpose as the source and ground of Christian life is essential to the piety of Calvin.

Calvin concluded the *Institutes* with the doctrine of the church, the community in which the Christian faith is lived. We are not angels, and we need the mutual support of the communion of the saints. To be Christian is to share in the common life of the people of God.

John Calvin lived with the vivid awareness that the essential business of human life is having to do with the living God. He shared with all people, as his writings reveal, the struggle of faith and the weaknesses of the spirit. Yet he never faltered in affirming that his life had its origin in the purpose of God and that the chief end of life was not to save his own soul but to glorify God and to serve God in the world. He knew that human life can be fulfilled only when it is lived for that which is greater than life and which alone is worthy of life's highest devotion: the living God.

Note

1. The Form of Government of the Presbyterian Church (U.S.A.), chap. 1, sec. 3 (4).

I

The Christian Life

WE ARE NOT OUR OWN

We are not our own masters, but belong to God

Even though the law of the Lord provides the finest and best-disposed method of ordering a man's life, it seemed good to the Heavenly Teacher to shape his people by an even more explicit plan to that rule which he had set forth in the law. Here, then, is the beginning of this plan: the duty of believers is "to present their bodies to God as a living sacrifice, holy and acceptable to him," and in this consists the lawful worship of him [Rom. 12:1]. From this is derived the basis of the exhortation that "they be not conformed to the fashion of this world, but be transformed by the renewal of their minds, so that they may prove what is the will of God" [Rom. 12:2]. Now the great thing is this: we are consecrated and dedicated to God in order that we may thereafter think, speak, meditate, and do nothing except to his glory. For a sacred thing may not be applied to profane uses without marked injury to him.

If we, then, are not our own [cf. 1 Cor. 6:19] but the

Lord's, it is clear what error we must flee, and whither we must direct all the acts of our life.

We are not our own: let not our reason nor our will, therefore, sway our plans and deeds. We are not our own: let us therefore not set it as our goal to seek what is expedient for us according to the flesh. We are not our own: in so far as we can, let us therefore forget ourselves and all that is ours.

Conversely, we are God's: let us therefore live for him and die for him. We are God's: let his wisdom and will therefore rule all our actions. We are God's: let all the parts of our life accordingly strive toward him as our only lawful goal [Rom. 14:8; cf. 1 Cor. 6:19]. O, how much has that man profited who, having been taught that he is not his own, has taken away dominion and rule from his own reason that he may yield it to God! For, as consulting our self-interest is the pestilence that most effectively leads to our destruction, so the sole haven of salvation is to be wise in nothing and to will nothing through ourselves but to follow the leading of the Lord alone.

Let this therefore be the first step, that a man depart from himself in order that he may apply the whole force of his ability in the service of the Lord. I call "service" not only what lies in obedience to God's Word but what turns the mind of man, empty of its own carnal sense, wholly to the bidding of God's Spirit. While it is the first entrance to life, all philosophers were ignorant of this transformation, which Paul calls "renewal of the mind" [Eph. 4:23]. For they set up reason alone as the ruling principle in man, and think that it alone should be listened to; to it alone, in short, they entrust the conduct of life. But the Christian philosophy bids reason give way to, submit and subject itself to, the Holy Spirit so that the man himself may no longer live but hear Christ living and reigning within him [Gal. 2:20].

Institutes III. 7:1

SELF-DENIAL

Self-denial through devotion to God

From this also follows this second point: that we seek not the things that are ours but those which are of the Lord's will and will serve to advance his glory. This is also evidence of great progress: that, almost forgetful of ourselves, surely subordinating our self-concern, we try faithfully to devote our zeal to God and his commandments. For when Scripture bids us leave off self-concern, it not only erases from our minds the yearnings to possess, the desire for power, and the favor of men, but it also uproots ambition and all craving for human glory and other more secret plagues. Accordingly, the Christian must surely be so disposed and minded that he feels within himself it is with God he has to deal throughout his life. In this way, as he will refer all he has to God's decision and judgment, so will he refer his whole intention of mind scrupulously to him. For he who has learned to look to God in all things that he must do, at the same time avoids all vain thoughts. This, then, is that denial of self which Christ enjoins with such great earnestness upon his disciples at the outset of their service [cf. Matt. 16:24]. When it has once taken possession of their hearts, it leaves no place at all first either to pride, or arrogance, or ostentation; then either to avarice, or desire, or lasciviousness, or effeminacy, or to other evils that our self-love spawns [cf. 2 Tim. 3:2–5]. On the other hand, wherever denial of ourselves does not reign, there either the foulest vices rage without shame or if there is any semblance of virtue, it is vitiated by depraved lusting after glory. Show me a man, if you can, who, unless he has according to the commandment of the Lord renounced himself, would freely exercise goodness among men. For all who have not been possessed with this feeling have at least followed virtue for the sake of praise. Now those of the philosophers who at any time most strongly contended that virtue should be pursued for its own sake were puffed up with such great arrogance as to show they sought after virtue for no other reason than to have occasion for pride. Yet God is so displeased, both with those who court the popular breeze and with such swollen souls, as to declare that they have received their reward in this world [Matt. 6:2,5,16], and to make harlots and publicans nearer to the Kingdom of Heaven than are they [Matt. 21:31]. . . .

Self-denial gives us the right attitude toward our fellow men

Now in these words we perceive that denial of self has regard partly to men, partly—and chiefly—to God.

For when Scripture bids us act toward men so as to esteem them above ourselves [Phil. 2:3], and in good faith to apply ourselves wholly to doing them good [cf. Rom. 12:10], it gives us commandments of which our mind is quite incapable unless our mind be previously emptied of its natural feeling. For, such is the blindness with which we all rush into self-love that each one of us seems to himself to have just cause to be proud of himself and to despise all others in comparison. If God has conferred upon us anything of which we need not repent, relying upon it we immediately lift up our minds, and are not only puffed up but almost burst with pride. The very vices that infest us we take pains to hide from others, while we flatter ourselves with the pretense that they are slight and insignificant, and even sometimes embrace them as virtues. If others manifest the same endowments we admire in ourselves, or even superior ones, we spitefully belittle and revile these gifts in order to avoid yielding place to such persons. If there are any faults in others, not content with noting them with severe and sharp reproach, we hatefully exaggerate them. Hence arises such insolence that each one of us, as if exempt from the common lot, wishes to tower above the rest, and loftily and savagely abuses every mortal man, or at least looks down upon him as an inferior. The poor yield to the rich; the common folk, to the nobles; the servants, to their masters; the unlearned, to the educated. But there is no one who does not cherish within himself some opinion of his own pre-eminence.

Thus each individual, by flattering himself, bears a kind of kingdom in his breast. For claiming as his own what pleases him, he censures the character and morals of others. But if this comes to the point of conflict, his venom bursts forth. For many obviously display some gentleness so long as they find everything sweet and pleasant. But just how many are there who will preserve this even tenor of modesty when they are pricked and irritated? There is no other remedy than to tear out from our inward parts this most deadly pestilence of love of strife and love of self, even as it is plucked out by Scriptural teaching. For thus we are instructed to remember that those talents which God has bestowed upon us are not our own goods but the free gifts of God; and any persons who become proud of them show their ungratefulness. "Who causes you to excel?" Paul asks. "If you have received all things, why do you boast as if they were not given to you?" [1 Cor. 4:7].

Let us, then, unremittingly examining our faults, call ourselves back to humility. Thus nothing will remain in us to puff us up; but there will be much occasion to be cast down. On the other hand, we are bidden so to esteem and regard whatever gifts of God we see in other men that we may honor those men in whom they reside. For it would be great depravity on our part to deprive them of that honor which the Lord has bestowed upon them. But we are taught to overlook their faults, certainly not flatteringly to cherish them; but not on account of such faults to revile men whom we ought to cherish with good will and and honor. Thus it will come about that, whatever man we deal with, we shall treat him not only moderately and modestly but also cordially and as a friend. You will never attain true gentleness except by one path: a heart imbued with lowliness and with reverence for others.

Self-renunciation leads to proper helpfulness toward our neighbors

Now, in seeking to benefit one's neighbor, how difficult it is to do one's duty! Unless you give up all thought of self and, so to speak, get out of yourself, you will accomplish nothing here. For how can you perform those works which Paul teaches to be the works of love, unless you renounce yourself, and give yourself wholly to others? "Love," he says, "is patient and kind, not jealous or boastful, is not envious or puffed up, does not seek its own, is not irritable . . ." [1 Cor. 13: 4–5]. If this is the one thing required—that we seek not what is our own—still we shall do no little violence to nature, which so inclines us to love ourselves alone that it does not easily allow us to neglect ourselves and our possessions in order to look after another's good, nay, to yield willingly what is ours by right and resign it to another. But Scripture, to lead us by the hand to this, warns that whatever benefits we obtain from the Lord have been entrusted to us on this condition: that they be applied to the common good of the church. And therefore the lawful use of all benefits consists in a liberal and kindly sharing of them with others. No surer rule and no more valid exhortation to keep it could be devised than when we are taught that all the gifts we possess have been bestowed by God and entrusted to us on condition that they be distributed for our neighbors' benefit [cf. 1 Peter 4:10].

But Scripture goes even farther by comparing them to the powers with which the members of the human body are endowed [1 Cor. 12:12ff.]. No member has this power for itself nor applies it to its own private use; but each pours it out to the fellow members. Nor does it take any profit from its power except what proceeds from the common advantage of the whole body. So, too, whatever a godly man can do he ought to be able to do for his brothers, providing for himself in no way other than to have his mind intent upon the common upbuilding of the church. Let this, therefore, be our rule for generosity and beneficence: We are the stewards of everything God has conferred on us by which we are able to help our neighbor, and are required to render account of our stewardship. Moreover, the only right stewardship is that which is tested by the rule of love. Thus it will come about that we shall not only join zeal for another's benefit with care for our own advantage, but shall subordinate the latter to the former. . . .

Self-denial toward God: devotion to his will!

Let us reiterate in fuller form the chief part of self-denial, which, as we have said, looks to God. . . . It will be enough to show how it forms us to fair-mindedness and tolerance.

To begin with, then, in seeking either the convenience or the tranquility of the present life, Scripture calls us to resign ourselves and all our possessions to the Lord's will, and to yield to him the desires of our hearts to be tamed and subjugated. To covet wealth and honors, to strive for authority, to heap up riches, to gather together all those follies which seem to make for magnificence and pomp, our lust is mad, our desire boundless. On the other hand, wonderful is our fear, wonderful our hatred, of poverty, lowly birth, and humble condition! And we are spurred to rid ourselves of them by every means. Hence we can see how uneasy in mind all those persons are who order their lives according to their own plan. We can see how artfully they strive— to the point of weariness—to obtain the goal of their ambition or avarice, while, on the other hand, avoiding poverty and a lowly condition.

In order not to be caught in such snares, godly men must hold to this path. First of all, let them neither desire nor hope for, nor contemplate, any other way of prospering than by the Lord's blessing. Upon this, then, let them safely and confidently throw themselves and rest. For however beautifully the flesh may seem to suffice unto itself, while it either strives by its own effort for honors and riches or relies upon its diligence, or is aided by the favor of men, yet it is certain that all these things are nothing; nor will we benefit at all, either by skill or by labor, except insofar as the Lord prospers them both. On the contrary, however, his blessing alone finds a way, even through all hindrances, to bring all things to a happy and favorable outcome for us; again, though entirely without it, to enable us to obtain some glory and opulence for ourselves (as we daily see impious men amassing great honors and riches), yet, inasmuch as those upon whom the curse of God rests taste not even the least particle of happiness, without this blessing we shall obtain nothing but what turns to our misfortune. For we ought by no means to desire what makes men more miserable.

Trust in God's blessing only

Therefore, suppose we believe that every means toward a prosperous and desirable outcome rests upon the blessing of God alone; and that, when this is absent, all sorts of misery and calamity dog us. It remains for us not greedily to strive after riches and honors—whether relying upon our own dexterity of wit or our own diligence, or depending upon the favor of men, or having confidence in vainly imagined fortune—but for us always to look to the Lord so that by his guidance we may be led to whatever lot he has provided for us. Thus it will first come to pass that we shall not dash out to seize upon riches and usurp honors through wickedness and by stratagems and evil arts, or greed, to the injury of our neighbors; but pursue only those enterprises which do not lead us away from innocence.

Who can hope for the help of a divine blessing amidst frauds, robberies, and other wicked arts? For as that blessing follows only him who thinks purely and acts rightly, thus it calls back from crooked thoughts and wicked actions all those who seek it. Then will a bridle be put on us that we may not burn with an immoderate desire to grow rich or ambitiously pant after honors. For with what shamelessness does a man trust that he will be helped by God to obtain those things which he desires contrary to God's Word? Away with the thought that God would abet with his blessing what he curses with his mouth! Lastly, if things do not go according to our wish and hope, we will still be restrained from impatience and loathing of our condition, whatever it may be. For we shall know that this is to murmur against God, by whose will riches and poverty, contempt and honor, are dispensed. To sum up, he who rests solely upon the blessing of God, as it has been here expressed, will neither strive with evil arts after those things which men customarily madly seek after, which he realizes will not profit him, nor will he, if things go well, give credit to himself or even to his diligence, or industry, or fortune. Rather, he will give God the credit as its Author. But if, while other men's affairs flourish, he makes but slight advancement, or even slips back, he will still bear his low estate with greater equanimity and moderation of mind than some profane person would bear a moderate success which merely does not correspond with his wish. For he indeed possesses a solace in which he may repose more peacefully than in the highest degree of wealth or power. Since this leads to his salvation, he considers that his affairs are ordained by the Lord. We see that David was so minded; while he follows God and gives himself over to his leading, he attests that he is like a child weaned from his mother's breast, and that he does not occupy himself with things too deep and wonderful for him [Ps. 131:1–2].

Self-denial helps us bear adversity

And for godly minds the peace and forbearance we have spoken of ought not to rest solely in this point; but it must also be extended to every occurrence to which the present life is subject. Therefore, he alone has duly denied himself who has so totally resigned himself to the Lord that he permits every part of his life to be governed by God's will. He who will be thus composed in mind, whatever happens, will not consider himself miserable nor complain of his lot with ill will toward God. How necessary this disposition is will appear if you weigh the many chance happenings to which we are subject. Various diseases repeatedly trouble us: now plague rages; now we are cruelly beset by the calamities of war; now ice and hail, consuming the year's expectation, lead to barrenness, which reduces us to poverty; wife, parents, children, neighbors, are snatched away by death; our house is burned by fire. It is on account of these occurrences that men curse their life, loathe the day of their birth, abominate heaven and the light of day, rail against God, and as they are eloquent in blasphemy, accuse him of injustice and cruelty. But in these matters the believer must also look to God's kindness and truly fatherly indulgence. Accordingly, if he sees his house reduced to solitude by the removal of his kinsfolk, he will not indeed even then cease to bless the Lord, but rather will turn his attention to this thought: nevertheless, the grace of the Lord, which dwells in my house, will not leave it desolate. Or, if his crops are blasted by frost, or destroyed by ice, or beaten down with hail, and he sees famine threatening, yet he will not despair or bear a grudge against God, but will remain firm in this trust [cf. Ps. 78:47]: "Nevertheless we are in the Lord's protection, sheep brought up in his pastures" [Ps. 79:13]. The Lord will therefore supply food to us even in extreme barrenness. If he shall be afflicted by disease, he will not even then be so unmanned by the harshness of pain as to break forth into impatience and expostulate with God; but, by considering the righteousness and gentleness of God's chastening, he will recall himself to forebearance. In short, whatever happens, because he will know it ordained of God, he will undergo it with a peaceful and grateful mind so as not obstinately to resist the command of him into whose power he once for all surrendered himself and his every possession.

Especially let that foolish and most miserable consolation of the pagans be far away from the breast of the Christian man; to strengthen their minds against adversities they charged these to fortune. Against fortune they considered it foolish to be angry because she was blind and unthinking, with unseeing eyes wounding the deserving and the undeserving at the same time. On the contrary, the rule of piety is that God's hand alone is the judge and governor of fortune, good or bad, and that it does not rush about with heedless force, but with most orderly justice deals out good as well as ill to us.

Institutes III. 7:2, 4, 5, 8–10

BEARING THE CROSS

Christ's cross and ours

But it behooves the godly mind to climb still higher, to the height to which Christ calls his disciples: that each must bear his own cross [Matt. 16:24]. For whomever the Lord has adopted and deemed worthy of his fellowship ought to prepare themselves for a hard, toilsome, and unquiet life, crammed with very many and various kinds of evil. It is the Heavenly Father's will thus to exercise them so as to put his own children to a definite test. Beginning with Christ, his first-born, he follows this plan with all his children. For even though that Son was beloved above the rest, and in him the Father's mind was well pleased [Matt. 3:17 and 17:5], yet we see that far from being treated indulgently or softly, to speak the truth, while he dwelt on earth he was not only tried by a perpetual cross but his whole life was nothing but a sort of perpetual cross. The apostle notes the reason: that it behooved him to "learn obedience through what he suffered" [Heb. 5:8].

The cross leads us to perfect trust in God's power

Besides this, our Lord had no need to undertake the bearing of the cross except to attest and prove his obedience to the Father. But as for us, there are many reasons why we must pass our lives under a continual cross. First, as we are by nature too inclined to attribute everything to our flesh—unless our feebleness be shown, as it were, to our eyes—we readily esteem our virtue above its due measure. And we do not doubt, whatever happens, that against all difficulties it will remain unbroken and unconquered. Hence we are lifted up into stupid and empty confidence in the flesh; and relying on it, we are then insolently proud against God himself, as if our own powers were sufficient without his grace.

He can best restrain this arrogance when he proves to us by experience not only the great incapacity but also the frailty under which we labor. Therefore, he afflicts us either with disgrace or poverty, or bereavement, or disease, or other calamities. Utterly unequal to bearing these, insofar as they touch us, we soon succumb to them. Thus humbled, we learn to call upon his power, which alone makes us stand fast under the weight of afflictions. But even the most holy persons, however much they may recognize that they stand not through their own strength but through God's grace, are too sure of their own fortitude and constancy unless by the testing of the cross he bring them into a deeper knowledge of himself.

The cross trains us to patience and obedience

The Lord also has another purpose for afflicting his people: to test their patience and to instruct them to obedience. Not that they can manifest any other obedience to him save what he has given them. But it so pleases him by unmistakable proofs to make manifest and clear the graces which he has conferred upon the saints, that these may not lie idle, hidden within. Therefore, by bringing into the open the power and constancy to forebear, with which he has endowed his servants, he is said to test their patience. . . .

But if God himself does right in providing occasion to stir up those virtues which he has conferred upon his believers in order that they may not be hidden in obscurity—nay, lie useless and pass away—the afflictions of the saints, without which they would have no forbearance, are amply justified. They are also, I assert, instructed by the cross to obey, because thus they are taught to live not according to their own whim but according to God's will. Obviously, if everything went according to their own liking, they would not know what it is to follow God.

Suffering for righteousness' sake

Now, to suffer persecution for righteousness' sake is a singular comfort. For it ought to occur to us how much honor God bestows upon us in thus furnishing us with the special badge of his soldiery. I say that not only they who labor for the defense of the gospel but they who in any way maintain the cause of righteousness suffer persecution for righteousness. Therefore, whether in declaring God's truth against Satan's falsehoods or in taking up the protection of the good and the innocent against the wrongs of the wicked, we must undergo the offenses and hatred of the world, which may imperil either our life, our fortunes, or our honor. Let us not grieve or be troubled in thus far devoting our efforts to God, or count ourselves miserable in those matters in which he has with his own lips declared us blessed [Matt. 5:10]. Even poverty, if it be judged in itself, is misery; likewise exile, contempt, prison, disgrace; finally, death itself is the ultimate of all calamities. But when the favor of our God breathes upon us, every one of these things turns into happiness for us. We ought accordingly to be content with the testimony of Christ rather than with the false estimation of the flesh. So it will come about that we shall rejoice after the apostle's example, "whenever he will count us worthy to suffer dishonor for his name" [Acts 5:41]. What then? If, being innocent and of good conscience, we are stripped of our possessions by the wickedness of impious folk, we are indeed reduced to penury among men. But in God's presence in heaven our true riches are thus increased. If we are cast out of our own house, then we will be the more intimately received into God's family.

Patience according to philosophic and Christian understanding

Now, since we have taken the prime reason for bearing the cross from the contemplation of the divine will, we must define in a few words the difference between philosophic and Christian patience. Certainly, very few philosophers have climbed to such a height of reason as to understand that through afflictions we are tested by the hand of God, and to reckon that in this respect we must obey God. But they also advance no other reason than that it must be so. What else is this but to say that you must yield to God because it is vain for you to try to resist him? For if we obey God only because it is necessary, if we should be allowed to escape, we will cease to obey him. But Scripture bids us contemplate in the will of God something far different: namely, first righteousness and equity, then concern for our own salvation. Of this sort, then, are Christian exhortations to patience. Whether poverty or exile, or prison, or insult, or disease, or bereavement, or anything like them torture us, we must think that none of these things happens except by the will and providence of God, that he does nothing except with a well-ordered justice. What then? Do not our innumerable and daily offenses deserve to be chastised more severely and with heavier rods than the afflictions he lays upon us out of his kindness? Is it not perfectly fair that our flesh be tamed and made accustomed, as it were, to the yoke, lest it lustfully rage according to its own inward nature? Are not God's right and truth worth our trouble? But if God's undoubted equity appears in afflictions, we cannot either murmur or wrestle against it without iniquity. Now we do not hear that barren incantation, "We must yield because it is necessary," but a living and fully effective precept, "We must obey because it is unlawful to resist; we must bear patiently, since impatience would be insolence against God's righteousness."

Now, because that only is pleasing to us which we recognize to be for our salvation and good, our most merciful Father consoles us also in this respect when he asserts that in the very act of afflicting us with the cross he is providing for our salvation. But if it be clear that our afflictions are for our benefit, why should we not undergo them with a thankful and quiet mind?

Therefore, in patiently suffering these tribulations, we do not yield to necessity but we consent for our own good. These thoughts, I say, bring it to pass that, however much in bearing the cross our minds are constrained by the natural feeling of bitterness, they are as much diffused with spiritual joy. From this, thanksgiving also follows, which cannot exist without joy; but if the praise of the Lord and thanksgiving can come forth only from a cheerful and happy heart—and there is nothing that ought to interrupt this in us—it thus is

clear how necessary it is that the bitterness of the cross
be tempered with spiritual joy.

Institutes III. 8:1, 2, 4, 7, 11

MEDITATION ON THE FUTURE LIFE

The vanity of this life

Whatever kind of tribulation presses upon us, we
must ever look to this end: to accustom ourselves to
contempt for the present life and to be aroused thereby
to meditate upon the future life. For since God knows
best how much we are inclined by nature to a brutish
love of this world, he uses the fittest means to draw us
back and to shake off our sluggishness, lest we cleave
too tenaciously to that love. There is not one of us,
indeed, who does not wish to seem throughout his life
to aspire and strive after heavenly immortality. For it
is a shame for us to be no better than brute beasts,
whose condition would be no whit inferior to our own
if there were not left to us hope of eternity after death.
But if you examine the plans, the efforts, the deeds, of
anyone, there you will find nothing else but earth.
Now our blockishness arises from the fact that our
minds, stunned by the empty dazzlement of riches,
power, and honors, become so deadened that they can
see no farther. The heart also, occupied with avarice,
ambition, and lust, is so weighed down that it cannot
rise up higher. In fine, the whole soul, enmeshed in the
allurements of the flesh, seeks its happiness on earth.
To counter this evil the Lord instructs his followers in

20

the vanity of the present life by continual proof of its miseries. Therefore, that they may not promise themselves a deep and secure peace in it, he permits them often to be troubled and plagued either with wars or tumults, or robberies, or other injuries. That they may not pant with too great eagerness after fleeting and transient riches, or repose in those which they possess, he sometimes by exile, sometimes by barrenness of the earth, sometimes by fire, sometimes by other means, reduces them to poverty, or at least confines them to a moderate station. . . . But if, in all these matters, he is more indulgent toward them, yet, that they may not either be puffed up with vainglory or exult in self-assurance, he sets before their eyes, through diseases and perils, how unstable and fleeting are all the goods that are subject to mortality.

Then only do we rightly advance by the discipline of the cross when we learn that this life, judged in itself, is troubled, turbulent, unhappy in countless ways, and in no respect clearly happy; that all those things which are judged to be its goods are uncertain, fleeting, vain, and vitiated by many intermingled evils. From this, at the same time, we conclude that in this life we are to seek and hope for nothing but struggle; when we think of our crown, we are to raise our eyes to heaven. For this we must believe: that the mind is never seriously aroused to desire and ponder the life to come unless it be previously imbued with contempt for the present life.

Gratitude for earthly life!

But let believers accustom themselves to a contempt of the present life that engenders no hatred of it or ingratitude against God. Indeed, this life, however crammed with infinite miseries it may be, is still rightly to be counted among those blessings of God which are not to be spurned. Therefore, if we recognize in it no divine benefit, we are already guilty of grave ingratitude toward God himself. For believers especially, this ought to be a testimony of divine benevolence, wholly destined, as it is, to promote their salvation. For before he shows us openly the inheritance of eternal glory, God wills by lesser proofs to show himself to be our Father. These are the benefits that are daily conferred on us by him. Since, therefore, this life serves us in understanding God's goodness, should we despise it as if it had no grain of good in itself? We must, then, become so disposed and minded that we count it among those gifts of divine generosity which are not at all to be rejected. For if testimonies of Scripture were lacking, and they are very many and very clear, nature itself also exhorts us to give thanks to the Lord because he has brought us into its light, granted us the use of it, and provided all the necessary means to preserve it.

And this is a much greater reason if in it we reflect that we are in preparation, so to speak, for the glory of the Heavenly Kingdom. For the Lord has ordained that those who are one day to be crowned in heaven should first undergo struggles on earth in order that they may not triumph until they have overcome the difficulties of war, and attained victory.

Then there is another reason: we begin in the present life, through various benefits, to taste the sweetness of the divine generosity in order to whet our hope and desire to seek after the full revelation of this. When we are certain that the earthly life we live is a gift of God's kindness, as we are beholden to him for it we ought to remember it and be thankful. Then we shall come in good time to consider its most unhappy condition in order that we may, indeed, be freed from too much desire of it, to which, as has been said, we are of ourselves inclined by nature.

Against the fear of death!

But monstrous it is that many who boast themselves Christians are gripped by such a great fear of death, rather than a desire for it, that they tremble at the least mention of it, as of something utterly dire and disastrous. Surely, it is no wonder if the natural awareness in us bristles with dread at the mention of our dissolution. But it is wholly unbearable that there is not in Christian hearts any light of piety to overcome and suppress that fear, whatever it is, by a greater consolation. For if we deem this unstable, defective, corruptible, fleeting, wasting, rotting tabernacle of our body to be so dissolved that it is soon renewed unto a firm, perfect, incorruptible, and finally, heavenly glory, will not faith compel us ardently to seek what nature dreads? If we should think that through death we are recalled from exile to dwell in the fatherland, in the heavenly fatherland, would we get no comfort from this fact?

The comfort prepared for believers by aspiration for the life to come

This truly is our sole comfort. If it be taken away, either our minds must become despondent or, to our destruction, be captivated with the empty solace of this world. Even the prophet confesses that his steps had well-nigh wavered when he stopped too long to dwell upon the present prosperity of the wicked [Ps. 73:2–3], and he could not understand it until he entered God's sanctuary and gazed upon the ultimate end of the pious and the wicked [Ps. 73:17]. To conclude in a word: if believers' eyes are turned to the power of the resurrection, in their hearts the cross of Christ will at last triumph over the devil, flesh, sin, and wicked men.

Institutes III. 9:1, 3, 5, 6

HOW WE MUST USE THE PRESENT LIFE AND ITS HELPS

The good things of this life are to be enjoyed as gifts of God (1–2).

1. Double danger: mistaken strictness and mistaken laxity

By such elementary instruction, Scripture at the same time duly informs us what is the right use of earthly benefits—a matter not to be neglected in the ordering of our life. For if we are to live, we have also to use those helps necessary for living. And we also cannot avoid those things which seem to serve delight more than necessity. Therefore we must hold to a measure so as to use them with a clear conscience, whether for necessity or for delight. By his word the Lord lays down this measure when he teaches that the present life is for his people as a pilgrimage on which they are hastening toward the Heavenly Kingdom [Lev. 25:23; 1 Chron. 29:15; Ps. 39:13; 119:19; Heb. 11:8–10, 13–16; 13:14; 1 Peter 2:11]. If we must simply pass through this world, there is no doubt we ought to use its good things insofar as they help rather than hinder our course. Thus Paul rightly persuades us to use this world as if not using it; and to buy goods with the same attitude as one sells them [1 Cor. 7:31–30].

But, because this topic is a slippery one and slopes on both sides into error, let us try to plant our feet where we may safely stand. There were some otherwise good and holy men who when they saw intemperance and wantonness, when not severely restrained, ever raging with unbridled excess, desired to correct this dangerous evil. This one plan occurred to them: they allowed man to use physical goods insofar as necessity required. A godly counsel indeed, but they were far too severe. For they would fetter consciences more tightly than does the Word of the Lord—a very dangerous thing. Now, to them necessity means to abstain from all things that they could do without;

thus, according to them, it would scarcely be permitted to add any food at all to plain bread and water. And others are even more severe. We are told of Crates the Theban; that he cast all his goods into the sea; for he thought that unless they were destroyed, they would destroy him.

But many today, while they seek an excuse for the intemperance of the flesh in its use of external things, and while they would meanwhile pave the road to licentious indulgence, take for granted what I do not at all concede to them: that this freedom is not to be restrained by any limitation but to be left to every man's conscience to use as far as seems lawful to him. Certainly I admit that consciences neither ought to nor can be bound here to definite and precise legal formulas; but, inasmuch as Scripture gives general rules for lawful use, we ought surely to limit our use in accordance with them.

2. *The main principle*

Let this be our principle: that the use of God's gifts is not wrongly directed when it is referred to that end to which the Author himself created and destined them for us, since he created them for our good, not for our ruin. Accordingly, no one will hold to a straighter path than he who diligently looks to this end. Now if we ponder to what end God created food, we shall find that he meant not only to provide for necessity but also for delight and good cheer. Thus the purpose of clothing, apart from necessity, was comeliness and decency.

In grasses, trees, and fruits, apart from their various uses, there is beauty of appearance and pleasantness of odor [cf. Gen. 2:9]. For if this were not true, the prophet would not have reckoned them among the benefits of God, "that wine gladdens the heart of man, that oil makes his face shine" [Ps. 104:15]. Scripture would not have reminded us repeatedly, in commending his kindness, that he gave all such things to men. And the natural qualities themselves of things demonstrate sufficiently to what end and extent we may enjoy them. Has the Lord clothed the flowers with the great beauty that greets our eyes, the sweetness of smell that is wafted upon our nostrils, and yet will it be unlawful for our eyes to be affected by that beauty, or our sense of smell by the sweetness of that odor? What? Did he not so distinguish colors as to make some more lovely than others? What? Did he not endow gold and silver, ivory and marble, with a loveliness that renders them more precious than other metals or stones? Did he not, in short, render many things attractive to us, apart from their necessary use?

We are not to use these blessings indulgently, or to seek wealth greedily, but to serve dutifully in our calling (3–6).

3. A look at the Giver of the gift prevents narrow-mindedness and immoderation

Away, then, with that inhuman philosophy which, while conceding only a necessary use of creatures, not only malignantly deprives us of the lawful fruit of

God's beneficence but cannot be practiced unless it robs a man of all his senses and degrades him to a block.

But no less diligently, on the other hand, we must resist the lust of the flesh, which, unless it is kept in order, overflows without measure. And it has, as I have said, its own advocates, who, under the pretext of the freedom conceded, permit everything to it. First, one bridle is put upon it if it be determined that all things were created for us that we might recognize the Author and give thanks for his kindness toward us. Where is your thanksgiving if you so gorge yourself with banqueting or wine that you either become stupid or are rendered useless for the duties of piety and of your calling? Where is your recognition of God if your flesh boiling over with excessive abundance into vile lust infects the mind with its impurity so that you cannot discern anything that is right and honorable? Where is our gratefulness toward God for our clothing if in the sumptuousness of our apparel we both admire ourselves and despise others, if with its elegance and glitter we prepare ourselves for shameless conduct? Where is our recognition of God if our minds be fixed upon the splendor of our apparel? For many so enslave all their senses to delights that the mind lies overwhelmed. Many are so delighted with marble, gold, and pictures that they become marble, they turn, as it were, into metals and are like painted figures. The smell of the kitchen or the sweetness of its odors so stupefies others that they are unable to smell anything spiritual. The same thing is also to be seen in other matters. Therefore, clearly, leave to abuse God's gifts must be somewhat curbed, and Paul's rule is confirmed: that we should "make no provision for the flesh, to gratify its desires" [Rom. 13:14], for if we yield too much to these, they boil up without measure or control.

4. Aspiration to eternal life also determines aright our outward conduct of life

But there is no surer or more direct course than that which we receive from contempt of the present life and meditation upon heavenly immortality. For from this two rules follow: those who use this world should be so affected as if they did not use it; those who marry, as if they did not marry; those who buy, as if they did not buy, just as Paul enjoins [1 Cor. 7:29–31]. The other rule is that they should know how to bear poverty peaceably and patiently, as well as to bear abundance moderately. He who bids you use this world as if you used it not destroys not only the intemperance of gluttony in food and drink, and excessive indulgence at table, in buildings and clothing, ambition, pride, arrogance, and overfastidiousness, but also all care and inclination that either diverts or hinders you from thought of the heavenly life and zeal to cultivate the soul. Long ago, Cato truly said: "There is great care about dress, but great carelessness about virtue." To use the old proverb: those who are much occupied with the care of the body are for the most part careless about their own souls.

Therefore, even though the freedom of believers in

external matters is not to be restricted to a fixed formula, yet it is surely subject to this law: to indulge oneself as little as possible; but, on the contrary, with unflagging effort of mind to insist upon cutting off all show of superfluous wealth, not to mention licentiousness, and diligently to guard against turning helps into hindrances.

5. Frugality: earthly possessions held in trust

The second rule will be: they who have narrow and slender resources should know how to go without things patiently, lest they be troubled by an immoderate desire for them. If they keep this rule of moderation, they will make considerable progress in the Lord's school. So, too, they who have not progressed, in some degree at least, in this respect have scarcely anything to prove them disciples of Christ. For besides the fact that most other vices accompany the desire for earthly things, he who bears poverty impatiently also when in prosperity commonly betrays the contrary disease. This is my point: he who is ashamed of mean clothing will boast of costly clothing; he who, not content with a slender meal, is troubled by the desire for a more elegant one, will also intemperately abuse those elegances if they fall to his lot. He who will bear reluctantly, and with a troubled mind, his deprivation and humble condition if he be advanced to honors will by no means abstain from arrogance. To this end, then, let all those for whom the pursuit of piety is not a pretense strive to learn, by the Apostle's example, how to be filled and to hunger, to abound and to suffer want [Phil. 4:12].

Besides, Scripture has a third rule with which to regulate the use of earthly things. Of it we said something when we discussed the precepts of love. It decrees that all those things were so given to us by the kindness of God, and so destined for our benefit, that they are, as it were, entrusted to us, and we must one day render account of them. Thus, therefore, we must so arrange it that this saying may continually resound in our ears: "Render account of your stewardship" [Luke 16:2]. At the same time let us remember by whom such reckoning is required: namely, him who has greatly commended abstinence, sobriety, frugality, and moderation, and has also abominated excess, pride, ostentation, and vanity; who approves no other distribution of good things than one joined with love; who has already condemned with his own lips all delights that draw man's spirit away from chastity and purity, or befog his mind.

6. The Lord's calling a basis of our way of life

Finally, this point is to be noted: the Lord bids each one of us in all life's actions to look to his calling. For he knows with what great restlessness human nature flames, with what fickleness it is borne hither and thither, how its ambition longs to embrace various things at once. Therefore, lest through our stupidity and rashness everything be turned topsy-turvy, he has appointed duties for every man in his particular way of life. And that no one may thoughtlessly transgress his limits, he has named these various kinds of living "callings." Therefore each individual has his own kind of living assigned to him by the Lord as a sort of sentry post so that he may not heedlessly wander about throughout life. Now, so necessary is this distinction that all our actions are judged in his sight by it, often, indeed, far otherwise than in the judgment of human and philosophical reason. No deed is considered more noble, even among philosophers, than to free one's country from tyranny. Yet a private citizen who lays his hand upon a tyrant is openly condemned by the Heavenly Judge [1 Sam. 24:7, 11; 26:9].

But I will not delay to list examples. It is enough if we know that the Lord's calling is in everything the beginning and foundation of well-doing. And if there is anyone who will not direct himself to it, he will never hold to the straight path in his duties. Perhaps, sometimes, he could contrive something laudable in appearance; but whatever it may be in the eyes of men, it will be rejected before God's throne. Besides, there will be no harmony among the several parts of his life. Accordingly, your life will then be best ordered when it is directed to this goal. For no one, impelled by his own rashness, will attempt more than his calling will permit, because he will know that it is not lawful to exceed its bounds. A man of obscure station will lead a private life ungrudgingly so as not to leave the rank in which he has been placed by God. Again, it will be no slight relief from cares, labors, troubles, and other burdens for a man to know that God is his guide in all these things. The magistrate will discharge his functions more willingly; the head of the household will confine himself to his duty; each man will bear and swallow the discomforts, vexations, weariness, and anxieties in his way of life, when he has been persuaded that the burden was laid upon him by God. From this will arise also a singular consolation: that no task will be so sordid and base, provided you obey your calling in it, that it will not shine and be reckoned very precious in God's sight.

Institutes III. 10

2

Christian Freedom

*Need for a right understanding of the Christian
doctrine of freedom*

We must now discuss Christian freedom. He who
proposes to summarize gospel teaching ought by no
means to omit an explanation of this topic. For it is a
thing of prime necessity, and apart from a knowledge
of it consciences dare undertake almost nothing without doubting; they hesitate and recoil from many
things; they constantly waver and are afraid. But freedom is especially an appendage of justification and is
of no little avail in understanding its power. . . .

For, as soon as Christian freedom is mentioned, either passions boil or wild tumults rise unless these
wanton spirits are opposed in time, who otherwise
most wickedly corrupt the best things. Some, on the
pretext of this freedom, shake off all obedience toward
God and break out into unbridled license. Others dis-
dain it, thinking that it takes away all moderation,
order, and choice of things. What should we do here,

hedged about with such perplexities? Shall we say good-by to Christian freedom, thus cutting off occasion for such dangers? But, as we have said, unless this freedom be comprehended, neither Christ nor gospel truth, nor inner peace of soul, can be rightly known. Rather, we must take care that so necessary a part of doctrine be not suppressed, yet at the same time, that those absurd objections which are wont to arise be met.

Freedom from the law

Christian freedom, in my opinion, consists of three parts. The first: that the consciences of believers, in seeking assurance of their justification before God, should rise above and advance beyond the law, forgetting all law righteousness. For since, as we have elsewhere shown, the law leaves no one righteous, either it excludes us from all hope of justification or we ought to be freed from it, and in such a way, indeed, that no account is taken of works. For he who thinks that in order to obtain righteousness he ought to bring some trifle of works is incapable of determining their measure and limit but makes himself debtor to the whole law. Removing, then, mention of law, and laying aside all consideration of works, we should, when justification is being discussed, embrace God's mercy alone, turn our attention from ourselves, and look only to Christ. For there the question is not how we may become righteous but how, being unrighteous and unworthy, we may be reckoned righteous. If consciences wish to attain any certainty in this matter, they ought to give no place to the law.

Nor can any man rightly infer from this that the law is superfluous for believers, since it does not stop teaching and exhorting and urging them to good, even though before God's judgment seat it has no place in their consciences. For, inasmuch as these two things are very different, we must rightly and conscientiously distinguish them. The whole life of Christians ought to be a sort of practice of godliness, for we have been called to sanctification [1 Thess. 4:7; cf. Eph. 1:4; 1 Thess. 4:3]. Here it is the function of the law, by warning men of their duty, to arouse them to a zeal for holiness and innocence. But, where consciences are worried how to render God favorable, what they will reply, and with what assurance they will stand should they be called to his judgment, there we are not to reckon what the law requires, but Christ alone, who surpasses all perfection of the law, must be set forth as righteousness. . . .

Freedom from the constraint of the law establishes the true obedience of believers

The second part, dependent upon the first, is that consciences observe the law, not as if constrained by the necessity of the law, but that freed from the law's yoke they willingly obey God's will. For since they dwell in perpetual dread so long as they remain under the sway of the law, they will never be disposed with eager readiness to obey God unless they have already been given this sort of freedom. . . .

Freedom in "things indifferent" with proofs from Romans

The third part of Christian freedom lies in this: regarding outward things that are of themselves "indifferent," we are not bound before God by any religious obligation preventing us from sometimes using them and other times not using them, indifferently. And the knowledge of this freedom is very necessary for us, for if it is lacking, our consciences will have no repose and there will be no end to superstitions. Today we seem to many to be unreasonable because we stir up discussion over the unrestricted eating of meat, use of holidays and of vestments, and such things, which seem to them vain frivolities.

But these matters are more important than is commonly believed. For when consciences once ensnare themselves, they enter a long and inextricable maze, not easy to get out of. If a man begins to doubt whether he may use linen for sheets, shirts, handkerchiefs, and napkins, he will afterward be uncertain also about hemp; finally, doubt will even arise over tow. For he will turn over in his mind whether he can sup without napkins, or go without a handkerchief. If any man should consider daintier food unlawful, in the end he will not be at peace before God, when he eats either black bread or common victuals, while it occurs to him that he could sustain his body on even coarser foods.

If he boggles at sweet wine, he will not with clear conscience drink even flat wine, and finally he will not dare touch water if sweeter and cleaner than other water. To sum up, he will come to the point of considering it wrong to step upon a straw across his path, as the saying goes.

Here begins a weighty controversy, for what is in debate is whether God, whose will ought to precede all our plans and actions, wishes us to use these things or those. As a consequence, some, in despair, are of necessity cast into a pit of confusion; others, despising God and abandoning fear of him, must make their own way in destruction, where they have none ready-made. For all those entangled in such doubts, wherever they turn, see offense of conscience everywhere present.

Freedom in the use of God's gifts for his purposes

"I know," says Paul, "that nothing is common" (taking "common" in the sense of "profane"), "but it is common for anyone who thinks it common" [Rom. 14:14]. With these words Paul subjects all outward things to our freedom, provided our minds are assured that the basis for such freedom stands before God. But if any superstitious opinion poses a stumbling block for us, things of their own nature pure are for us corrupt. For this reason, he adds: "Happy is he who does not judge himself in what he approves. But he who judges, if he eats, is condemned, because he does not eat of faith. For whatever is not of faith is sin" [Rom. 14: 22–23].

Amidst such perplexities, do not those who show themselves rather bold by daring all things confidently, nonetheless to this extent turn away from God? But they who are deeply moved in any fear of God, when they are compelled to commit many things against their conscience, are overwhelmed and fall down with fright. All such persons receive none of God's gifts with thanksgiving, yet Paul testifies that by this alone all things are sanctified for our use [1 Tim. 4:4–5]. Now I mean that thanksgiving which proceeds from a mind that recognizes in his gifts the kindness and goodness of God. For many of them, indeed, understand them as good things of God which they use, and praise God in his works; but inasmuch as they have not been persuaded that these good things have been given to them, how can they thank God as the giver?

To sum up, we see whither this freedom tends: namely, that we should use God's gifts for the purpose for which he gave them to us, with no scruple of conscience, no trouble of mind. With such confidence our minds will be at peace with him, and will recognize his liberality toward us. For here are included all ceremonies whose observance is optional, that our consciences may not be constrained by any necessity to observe them but may remember that by God's beneficence their use is for edification made subject to him.

Against the abuse of Christian freedom for gluttony and luxury!

But we must carefully note that Christian freedom is, in all its parts, a spiritual thing. Its whole force consists in quieting frightened consciences before God —that are perhaps disturbed and troubled over forgiveness of sins, or anxious whether unfinished works, corrupted by the faults of our flesh, are pleasing to God, or tormented about the use of things indifferent. Accordingly, it is perversely interpreted both by those who allege it as an excuse for their desires that they may abuse God's good gifts to their own lust and by those who think that freedom does not exist unless it is used before men, and consequently, in using it have no regard for weaker brethren.

Today men sin to a greater degree in the first way. There is almost no one whose resources permit him to be extravagant who does not delight in lavish and ostentatious banquets, bodily apparel, and domestic architecture; who does not wish to outstrip his neighbors in all sorts of elegance; who does not wonderfully flatter himself in his opulence. And all these things are defended under the pretext of Christian freedom. They say that these are things indifferent. I admit it, provided they are used indifferently. But when they are coveted too greedily, when they are proudly boasted of, when they are lavishly squandered, things that were of themselves otherwise lawful are certainly defiled by these vices.

Paul's statement best distinguishes among things indifferent: "To the clean all things are clean, but to the corrupt and unbelieving nothing is clean, inasmuch as their minds and consciences are corrupted" [Titus 1:15]. For why are the rich cursed, who have their consolation, who are full, who laugh now [Luke 6:24–25], who sleep on ivory couches [Amos 6:4], "who join field to field" [Isa. 5:8], whose feasts have harp, lyre, timbrel, and wine [Isa. 5:12]? Surely ivory and gold and riches are good creations of God, permitted, indeed appointed, for men's use by God's providence. And we have never been forbidden to laugh, or to be filled, or to join new possessions to old or ancestral ones, or to delight in musical harmony, or to drink wine. True, indeed. But where there is plenty, to wallow in delights, to gorge oneself, to intoxicate mind and heart with present pleasures and be always panting after new ones—such are very far removed from a lawful use of God's gifts.

Away, then, with uncontrolled desire, away with immoderate prodigality, away with vanity and arrogance—in order that men may with a clean conscience cleanly use God's gifts. Where the heart is tempered to this soberness they will have a rule for lawful use of such blessings. But should this moderation be lacking, even base and common pleasures are too much. It is a true saying that under coarse and rude attire there often dwells a heart of purple, while sometimes under silk and purple is hid a simple humility. Thus let every man live in his station, whether slenderly, or moderately, or plentifully, so that all may remember God nourishes them to live, not to luxuriate. And let them regard this as the law of Christian freedom; to have learned with Paul, in whatever state they are, to be content; to know how to be humble and exalted; to have been taught, in any and all circumstances, to be filled and to hunger, to abound and to suffer want [Phil. 4:11–12].

Against the abuse of Christian freedom to the injury of the weak!

In this respect also many err: they use their freedom indiscriminately and unwisely, as though it were not sound and safe if men did not witness it. By this heedless use, they very often offend weak brothers. You can see some persons today who reckon their freedom does not exist unless they take possession of it by eating meat on Fridays. I do not blame them for eating meat, but this false notion must be driven from their minds. For they ought to think that from their freedom they obtain nothing new in men's sight but before God, and that it consists as much in abstaining as in using. If they understand that it makes no difference in God's sight whether they eat meat or eggs, wear red or black clothes, this is enough and more. The conscience, to which the benefit of such freedom was due, is now set free. Consequently, even if men thereafter abstain from meat throughout life, and ever wear clothes of one color, they are not less free. Indeed, because they are free, they abstain with a free conscience. But in having no regard for their brothers' weakness they slip most disastrously, for we ought so to bear with it that we do not heedlessly allow what would do them the slightest harm.

But it is sometimes important for our freedom to be declared before men. This I admit. Yet we must with the greatest caution hold to this limitation, that we do not abandon the care of the weak, whom the Lord has so strongly commended to us.

On offenses

Here, then, I shall say something about offenses—how they are to be distinguished, which ones avoided, which overlooked. From this we may afterward be able to determine what place there is for our freedom among men. Now I like that common distinction between an offense given and one received, inasmuch as it has the clear support of Scripture and properly expresses what is meant.

If you do anything with unseemly levity, or wantonness, or rashness, out of its proper order or place, so as to cause the ignorant and the simple to stumble, such will be called an offense given by you, since by your fault it came about that this sort of offense arose. And, to be sure, one speaks of an offense as given in some matter when its fault arises from the doer of the thing itself.

An offense is spoken of as received when something, otherwise not wickedly or unseasonably committed, is by ill will or malicious intent of mind wrenched into occasion for offense. Here is no "given" offense, but those wicked interpreters baselessly so understand it. None but the weak is made to stumble by the first kind of offense, but the second gives offense to persons of bitter disposition and pharisaical pride. Accordingly, we shall call the one the offense of the weak, the other that of the Pharisees. Thus we shall so temper the use of our freedom as to allow for the ignorance of our weak brothers, but for the rigor of the Pharisees, not at all! . . .

On the right use of Christian freedom and the right renunciation of it

Still the matter will remain in doubt unless we grasp whom we are to consider weak, whom Pharisees. If this distinction is removed, I do not see what use for freedom really remains in relation to offenses, for it will always be in the greatest danger. But Paul seems to me most clearly to have defined, both by teaching and by example, how far our freedom must either be moderated or purchased at the cost of offenses. When Paul took Timothy into his company, he circumcised him [Acts 16:3.]. But he could not be brought to circumcise Titus [Gal. 2:3.]. Here was a diversity of acts but no change of purpose or mind. That is, in circumcising Timothy, although he was "free from all," he made himself "a slave to all"; and "to the Jews" he "became as a Jew" in order to win Jews; to those under the law he "became as one under the law . . . that" he "might win those under the law" [1 Cor. 9:19–20]; "all things to all men that" he "might save many" [1 Cor. 9:22], as he elsewhere writes. We have due control over our freedom if it makes no difference to us to restrict it when it is fruitful to do so.

What he had in view when he strongly refused to circumcise Titus he testifies when he thus writes: "But even Titus, who was with me, was not compelled to be circumcised, though he was a Greek, but because of false brethren surreptitiously brought in, who slipped in to spy out our freedom, which we have in Christ Jesus, that they might bring us into bondage—to them we did not yield submission, even for a moment, that the truth of the gospel might be preserved among you" [Gal. 2:3–5]. We have need also to assert our freedom if through the unjust demands of false apostles it be endangered in weak consciences.

We must at all times seek after love and look toward the edification of our neighbor. "All things," he says elsewhere, "are lawful to me, but not all things are helpful. All things are lawful, but not all things build up. Let no one seek his own good but another's" [1 Cor. 10:23–24]. Nothing is plainer than this rule: that we should use our freedom if it results in the edification of our neighbor, but if it does not help our neighbor, then we should forgo it. There are those who pretend a Pauline prudence in abstaining from freedom, while there is nothing to which they apply it less than to the duties of love. To protect their own repose, they wish all mention of freedom to be buried; when it is no less important sometimes to use our neighbors' freedom for their good and edification than on occasion to restrain it for their own benefit. But it is the part of a godly man to realize that free power in outward matters has been given him in order that he may be the more ready for all the duties of love.

We must not on pretext of love of neighbor offend against God

All that I have taught about avoiding offenses I mean to be referred to things intermediate and indifferent. For the things necessary to be done must not be omitted for fear of any offense. For as our freedom must be subordinated to love, so in turn ought love itself to abide under purity of faith. Surely, it is fitting here also to take love into consideration, even as far as to the altar [cf. Matt. 5:23–24]; that is, that for our neighbor's sake we may not offend God.

Institutes III. 19:1, 2, 4, 5, 7–13

3

Prayer

TREATISE ON PRAYER

The necessity of prayer

It is . . . by the benefit of prayer that we reach those riches which are laid up for us with the Heavenly Father. For there is a communion of men with God by which, having entered the heavenly sanctuary, they appeal to him in person concerning his promises in order to experience, where necessity so demands, that what they believed was not vain, although he had promised it in word alone. Therefore we see that to us nothing is promised to be expected from the Lord, which we are not also bidden to ask of him in prayers. So true is it that we dig up by prayer the treasures that were pointed out by the Lord's gospel, and which our faith has gazed upon.

Words fail to explain how necessary prayer is, and in how many ways the exercise of prayer is profitable. Surely, with good reason the Heavenly Father affirms that the only stronghold of safety is in calling upon his name [cf. Joel 2:32]. By so doing we invoke the presence both of his providence, through which he watches over and guards our affairs, and of his power, through which he sustains us, weak as we are and well-nigh overcome, and of his goodness, through which he receives us, miserably burdened with sins, unto grace; and, in short, it is by prayer that we call him to reveal himself as wholly present to us. Hence comes an extraordinary peace and repose to our consciences. For having disclosed to the Lord the necessity that was pressing upon us, we even rest fully in the thought that none of our ills is hid from him who, we are convinced, has both the will and the power to take the best care of us.

Objection: Is prayer not superfluous? Six reasons for it

But, someone will say, does God not know, even without being reminded, both in what respect we are troubled and what is expedient for us, so that it may seem in a sense superfluous that he should be stirred up by our prayers—as if he were drowsily blinking or even sleeping until he is aroused by our voice? But they who thus reason do not observe to what end the Lord instructed his people to pray, for he ordained it not so much for his own sake as for ours. Now he wills—as is right—that his due be rendered to him, in the recognition that everything men desire and account conducive to their own profit comes from him, and in the attestation of this by prayers. But the profit of this sacrifice also, by which he is worshiped, returns to us.

Accordingly, the holy fathers, the more confidently they extolled God's benefits among themselves and others, were the more keenly aroused to pray. It will be enough for us to note the single example of Elijah, who, sure of God's purpose, after he has deliberately promised rain to King Ahab, still anxiously prays with his head between his knees, and sends his servant seven times to look [I Kings 18:42], not because he would discredit his prophecy, but because he knew it was his duty, lest his faith be sleepy or sluggish, to lay his desires before God.

Therefore, even though, while we grow dull and stupid toward our miseries, he watches and keeps guard on our behalf, and sometimes even helps us unasked, still it is very important for us to call upon him: First, that our hearts may be fired with a zealous and burning desire ever to seek, love, and serve him, while we become accustomed in every need to flee to him as to a sacred anchor. Secondly, that there may enter our hearts no desire and no wish at all of which we should be ashamed to make him a witness, while we learn to set all our wishes before his eyes, and even to pour out our whole hearts. Thirdly, that we be prepared to receive his benefits with true gratitude of heart and thanksgiving, benefits that our prayer reminds us come from his hand [cf. Ps. 145:15–16]. Fourthly, moreover, that, having obtained what we were seeking, and being convinced that he has answered our prayers, we should be led to meditate upon his kindness more ardently. And fifthly, that at the same time we embrace with greater delight those things which we acknowledge to have been obtained by prayers. Finally, that use and experience may, according to the measure of our feebleness, confirm his providence, while we understand not only that he promises never to fail us, and of his own will opens the way to call upon him at the very point of necessity, but also that he ever extends his hand to help his own, not wet-nursing them with words but defending them with present help. . . .

THE RULES OF RIGHT PRAYER

First Rule: Reverence.

Devout detachment required for conversation with God

Now for framing prayer duly and properly, let this be the first rule: that we be disposed in mind and heart as befits those who enter conversation with God. This we shall indeed attain with respect to the mind if it is freed from carnal cares and thoughts by which it can be called or led away from right and pure contemplation of God, and then not only devotes itself completely to prayer but also, insofar as this is possible, is lifted and carried beyond itself. Now I do not here require the mind to be so detached as never to be pricked or gnawed by vexations, since, on the contrary, great anxiety should kindle in us the desire to pray. Thus we see that God's saintly servants give proof of huge torments, not to say vexations, when they speak of uttering their plaintive cry to the Lord from the deep abyss, and from the very jaws of death [cf. Ps. 130:1]. But I say that we are to rid ourselves of all alien and outside cares, by which the mind, itself a wanderer, is borne about hither and thither, drawn away from heaven, and pressed down to earth. I mean that it ought to be raised above itself that it may not bring into God's sight anything our blind and stupid reason is wont to devise, nor hold itself within the limits of its own vanity, but rise to a purity worthy of God.

Against undisciplined and irreverent prayer

These two matters are well worth attention: first, whoever engages in prayer should apply to it his faculties and efforts, and not, as commonly happens, be distracted by wandering thoughts. For nothing is more contrary to reverence for God than the levity that marks an excess of frivolity utterly devoid of awe. In this matter, the harder we find concentration to be, the more strenuously we ought to labor after it. For no one is so intent on praying that he does not feel many irrelevant thoughts stealing upon him, which either break the course of prayer or delay it by some winding bypath. But here let us recall how unworthy it is, when God admits us to intimate conversation, to abuse his great kindness by mixing sacred and profane; but just as if the discourse were between us and an ordinary man, amidst our prayers we neglect him and flit about hither and thither.

Let us therefore realize that the only persons who duly and properly gird themselves to pray are those who are so moved by God's majesty that freed from earthly cares and affections they come to it. And the rite of raising the hands means that men remember they are far removed from God unless they raise their thoughts on high. As it is also said in the psalm: "To thee . . . I have lifted up my soul" [Ps. 25:1; cf. 24:1]. And Scripture quite often uses this expression, "to lift up prayer" [e.g., Isa. 37:4], in order that those who wish God to hear them may not settle down "on their lees" [cf. Jer. 48:11; Zeph. 1:12]. In short, the more generously God deals with us, gently summoning us to unburden our cares into his bosom, the less excusable are we if his splendid and incomparable benefit does not outweigh all else with us and draw us to him, so that we apply our minds and efforts zealously to prayer. This cannot happen unless the mind, stoutly wrestling with these hindrances, rises above them.

We have noted another point: not to ask any more than God allows. For even though he bids us pour out our hearts before him [Ps. 62:8; cf. Ps. 145:19], he still does not indiscriminately slacken the reins to stupid and wicked emotions; and while he promises that he will act according to the will of the godly, his gentleness does not go so far that he yields to their willfulness. Yet in both, men commonly sin gravely; for many rashly, shamelessly, and irreverently dare importune God with their improprieties and impudently present before his throne whatever in dreams has struck their fancy. But such great dullness or stupidity grips them that they dare thrust upon God all their vilest desires, which they would be deeply ashamed to acknowledge to men. . . .

The Holy Spirit aids right prayer

But because our abilities are far from able to match such perfection, we must seek a remedy to help us. As we must turn keenness of mind toward God, so affection of heart has to follow. Both, indeed, stand far beneath; nay, more truly, they faint and fail, or are carried in the opposite direction. Therefore, in order to minister to this weakness, God gives us the Spirit as our teacher in prayer, to tell us what is right and temper our emotions. For, "because we do not know how to pray as we ought, the Spirit comes to our help," and "intercedes for us with unspeakable groans" [Rom. 8:26]; not that he actually prays or groans but arouses in us assurance, desires, and sighs, to conceive which our natural powers would scarcely suffice. And Paul, with good reason, calls "unspeakable" these groans which believers give forth under the guidance of the Spirit; for they who are truly trained in prayers are not unmindful that, perplexed by blind anxieties, they are so constrained as scarcely to find out what it is expedient for them to utter. Indeed, when they try to stammer, they are confused and hesitate. Clearly, then, to pray rightly is a rare gift. These things are not said in order that we, favoring our own slothfulness, may give over the function of prayer to the Spirit of God, and vegetate in that carelessness to which we are all too prone. In this strain we hear the impious voices of certain persons, saying that we should drowsily wait until he overtake our preoccupied minds. But rather our intention is that, loathing our inertia and dullness, we should seek such aid of the Spirit. And indeed, Paul, when he enjoins us to pray in the Spirit [1 Cor. 14:15], does not stop urging us to watchfulness. He means that the prompting of the Spirit empowers us so to compose prayers as by no means to hinder or hold back our own effort, since in this matter God's will is to test how effectually faith moves our hearts.

Second Rule: We pray from a sincere sense of want, and with penitence.
The sense of need that excludes all unreality
Let this be the second rule: that in our petitions we ever sense our own insufficiency, and earnestly pondering how we need all that we seek, join with this prayer an earnest—nay, burning—desire to attain it. For many perfunctorily intone prayers after a set form, as if discharging a duty to God. And although they admit it to be a necessary remedy for their ills, because it would be fatal to lack the help of God which they are beseeching, still it appears that they perform this duty from habit, because their hearts are meanwhile cold, and they do not ponder what they ask. Indeed, a general and confused feeling of their need leads them to prayer, but it does not arouse them, as it were in present reality, to seek the relief of their poverty. Now what do we account more hateful or even execrable to God than the fiction of someone asking pardon for his

sins, all the while either thinking he is not a sinner or at least not thinking he is a sinner? Unquestionably something in which God himself is mocked! Yet, as I have just said, mankind is so stuffed with such depravity that for the sake of mere performance men often beseech God for many things that they are dead sure will, apart from his kindness, come to them from some other source, or already lie in their possession.

A fault that seems less serious but is also not tolerable is that of others who, having been imbued with this one principle—that God must be appeased by devotions—mumble prayers without meditation. Now the godly must particularly beware of presenting themselves before God to request anything unless they yearn for it with sincere affection of heart, and at the same time desire to obtain it from him. Indeed, even though in those things which we seek only to God's glory we do not seem at first glance to be providing for our own need, yet it is fitting that they be sought with no less ardor and eagerness. When, for example, we pray that "his name be sanctified" [Matt. 6:9; Luke 11:2], we should, so to speak, eagerly hunger and thirst after that sanctification. . . .

Third Rule: We yield all confidence in ourselves and humbly plead for pardon.

We come as humble suppliants for mercy

To this let us join a third rule: that anyone who stands before God to pray, in his humility giving glory completely to God, abandon all thought of his own glory, cast off all notion of his own worth, in fine, put away all self-assurance—lest if we claim for ourselves anything, even the least bit, we should become vainly puffed up, and perish at his presence. . . .

The plea for forgiveness of sins as the most important part of prayer

To sum up: the beginning, and even the preparation, of proper prayer is the plea for pardon with a humble and sincere confession of guilt. Nor should anyone, however holy he may be, hope that he will obtain anything from God until he is freely reconciled to him; nor can God chance to be propitious to any but those whom he has pardoned. Accordingly, it is no wonder if believers open for themselves the door to prayer with this key, as we learn from numerous passages of The Psalms. For David, asking for something else than remission of his sins, says: "Remember not the sins of my youth, and my transgressions; according to thy mercy remember me, for thy goodness' sake, O Lord" [Ps. 25:7]. Again: "See my affliction and my toil, and forgive all my sins" [Ps. 25:18]. Also, in this we see that it is not enough for us to call ourselves to account each day for recent sins if we do not remember those sins which might seem to have been long forgotten.

For the same prophet, elsewhere having confessed one grave offense, on this occasion even turns back to his mother's womb, in which he had contracted the infection [Ps. 51:5], not to extenuate the guilt on the ground of corruption of nature but that, in gathering up the sins of his whole life, the more rigorously he condemns himself, the more easily entreated he may find God. But even though the saints do not always beg forgiveness of sins in so many words, if we diligently ponder their prayers that Scripture relates, we shall readily come upon what I speak of: that they have received their intention to pray from God's mercy alone, and thus always have begun with appeasing him. For if anyone should question his own conscience, he would be so far from daring intimately to lay aside his cares before God that, unless he relied upon mercy and pardon, he would tremble at every approach.

There is also another special confession when suppliants ask release from punishments. It is that at the same time they may pray for the pardon of their sins. For it would be absurd to wish the effect to be removed while the cause remained. We must guard against imitating foolish sick folk, who, concerned solely with the treatment of symptoms, neglect the very root of the disease. We must make it our first concern that God be favorable toward us, rather than that he attest his favor by outward signs, because he wills to maintain this order, and it would have been of small profit to us to have him do us good unless our conscience, feeling him wholly appeased, rendered him altogether lovely [Cant. 5:16]. Christ's reply also reminds us of this; for after he had decided to heal the paralytic, "Your sins," he said, "are forgiven you" [Matt. 9:2]. He thus arouses our minds to that which we ought especially to desire: that God may receive us into grace; then, that in aiding us he may set forth the fruit of reconciliation.

But besides that special confession of present guilt, with which believers plead for the remission of every sin and penalty, the general preface that gains favor for prayers must never be passed over, for unless they are founded in free mercy, prayers never reach God. John's statement can be applied to this: "If we confess our sins, he is faithful and just to forgive . . . , and cleanse us from all unrighteousness" [1 John 1:9]. For this reason, under the law prayers had to be consecrated with blood atonement [cf. Gen. 12:8; 26:25; 33:20; 1 Sam. 7:9] in order that they should be accepted, and that the people should thus be warned that they were unworthy of so great a privilege of honor until, purged of their defilement, they derived confidence in prayer solely from God's mercy. . . .

Fourth Rule: We pray with confident hope.
Hope and faith overcome fear

The fourth rule is: thus cast down and overcome by true humility, we should be nonetheless encouraged to pray by a sure hope that our prayer will be answered. These are indeed things apparently contrary: to join the firm assurance of God's favor to a sense of his just vengeance; yet, on the ground that God's goodness alone raises up those oppressed by their own evil deeds, they very well agree together. For, in accordance with our previous teaching that repentance and faith are companions joined together by an indissoluble bond, although one of these terrifies us while the other gladdens us, so also these two ought to be present together in prayers. And David briefly expresses this agreement when he says: "I through the abundance of thy goodness will enter thy house. I will worship toward the temple of thy holiness with fear" [Ps. 5:7]. Under God's goodness he includes faith, meantime not excluding fear. For not only does his majesty constrain us to reverence but through our own unworthiness, forgetting all pride and self-confidence, we are held in fear.

But "assurance" I do not understand to mean that which soothes our mind with sweet and perfect repose, releasing it from every anxiety. For to repose so peacefully is the part of those who, when all affairs are flowing to their liking, are touched by no care, burn with no desire, toss with no fear. But for the saints the occasion that best stimulates them to call upon God is when, distressed by their own need, they are troubled by the greatest unrest, and are almost driven out of their senses, until faith opportunely comes to their relief. For among such tribulations God's goodness so shines upon them that even when they groan with weariness under the weight of present ills, and also are troubled and tormented by the fear of greater ones, yet, relying upon his goodness, they are relieved of the difficulty of bearing them, and are solaced and hope for escape and deliverance. It is fitting therefore that the godly man's prayer arise from these two emotions, that it also contain and represent both. That is, that he groan under present ills and anxiously fear those to come, yet at the same time take refuge in God, not at all doubting he is ready to extend his helping hand. It is amazing how much our lack of trust provokes God if we request of him a boon that we do not expect.

Prayer and faith

Therefore nothing is more in harmony with the nature of prayers than that this rule be laid down and established for them: that they not break forth by chance but follow faith as guide. Christ calls this principle to the attention of all of us with this saying: "I say unto you, whatever you seek . . . , believe that you will receive it, and it will come to you" [Mark 11:24]. . . .

To sum up, it is faith that obtains whatever is granted to prayer. Such is the meaning of Paul's famous statement, which the unwise too little regard: "How will anyone call upon him in whom he has not believed? And who will believe unless he has heard?" [Rom. 10:14]. "Faith comes by hearing, and hearing from the Word of God" [Rom. 10:17]. For, deducing step by step the beginning of prayer from faith, he plainly asserts that God cannot be sincerely called upon by others than those to whom, through the preaching of the gospel, his kindness and gentle dealing have become known—indeed, have been intimately revealed. . . .

Our prayers can obtain an answer only through God's forgiveness

This also is worth noting: what I have set forth on the four rules of right praying is not so rigorously required that God will reject those prayers in which he finds neither perfect faith nor repentance, together with a warmth of zeal and petitions rightly conceived.

I have said that, although prayer is an intimate conversation of the pious with God, yet reverence and moderation must be kept, lest we give loose rein to miscellaneous requests, and lest we crave more than God allows; further, that we should lift up our minds to a pure and chaste veneration of him, lest God's majesty become worthless for us. . . .

The intercession of Christ.
Prayer in the name of Jesus

Since no man is worthy to present himself to God and come into his sight, the Heavenly Father himself, to free us at once from shame and fear, which might well have thrown our hearts into despair, has given us his Son, Jesus Christ our Lord, to be our advocate [1 John 2:1] and mediator with him [1 Tim. 2:5; cf. Heb. 8:6 and 9:15], by whose guidance we may confidently come to him, and with such an intercessor, trusting nothing we ask in his name will be denied us, as nothing can be denied to him by the Father. And to this must be referred all that we previously taught about faith. For just as the promise commends Christ the Mediator to us, so, unless the hope of obtaining our requests depends upon him, it cuts itself off from the benefit of prayer.

For as soon as God's dread majesty comes to mind, we cannot but tremble and be driven far away by the recognition of our own unworthiness, until Christ comes forward as intermediary, to change the throne of dreadful glory into the throne of grace. As the apostle also teaches how we should dare with all confidence to appear, to receive mercy, and to find grace in timely help [Heb. 4:16]. And as a rule has been established to call upon God, and a promise given that those who call upon him shall be heard, so too we are particularly bidden to call upon him in Christ's name; and we have the promise made that we shall obtain what we have asked in his name. "Hitherto," he says, "you have asked nothing in my name; ask and you will receive" [John 16:24]. "In that day you will ask in my name" [John 16:26], and "whatever you ask . . . I will do it that the Father may be glorified in the Son" [John 14:13].

Hence it is incontrovertibly clear that those who call upon God in another name than that of Christ obstinately flout his commands and count his will as nought —indeed, have no promise of obtaining anything. Indeed, as Paul says, "all God's promises find their yea and amen in him" [2 Cor. 1:20]. That is, they are confirmed and fulfilled. . . .

Kinds of prayer: private and public.
Private prayer

But even though prayer is properly confined to entreaties and supplications, there is such a close connection between petition and thanksgiving that they may conveniently be included under one name. For those kinds which Paul lists fall under the first part of this division [cf. 1 Tim. 2:1]. In asking and beseeching, we pour out our desires before God, seeking both those things which make for the extension of his glory and the setting forth of his name, and those benefits which conduce to our own advantage. In giving thanks, we celebrate with due praise his benefits toward us, and credit to his generosity every good that comes to us. David, therefore, has combined these two functions: "Call upon me in the day of need; I will deliver you, and you shall glorify me" [Ps. 50:15]. Scripture with good reason enjoins us to use both constantly. For as we have stated elsewhere, the weight of our poverty and the facts of experience proclaim that the tribulations which drive and press us from all sides are so many and so great that there is reason enough for us all continually to groan and sigh to God, and to beseech him as suppliants. For even if they be free of adversities, the guilt of their transgressions and the innumerable assaults of temptations ought still to goad even the holiest to seek a remedy. But in the sacrifice of praise and thanksgiving there can be no interruption without sin, since God does not cease to heap benefits upon benefits in order to impel us, though slow and lazy, to gratefulness. In short, we are well-nigh overwhelmed by so great and so plenteous an outpouring of benefactions, by so many and mighty miracles discerned wherever one looks, that we never lack reason and occasion for praise and thanksgiving.

And to explain these things somewhat more clearly,

since, as has already been sufficiently proved, all our hope and wealth so reside in God that neither we nor our possessions prosper unless we can have his blessing, we ought constantly to commit ourselves and all that we have to him [cf. James 4:14–15]. Then whatever we determine, speak, do, let us determine, speak, and do under his hand and will—in a word, under the hope of his help. . . .

Not only do God's benefits claim for themselves the extolling by the tongue, but also they naturally win love for themselves. "I loved the Lord," says David, "because he heard the voice of my supplication" [Ps. 116:1]. Also, elsewhere recounting what help he had experienced: "I shall love thee, O God, my strength" [Ps. 18:1]. But praises that do not flow from this sweetness of love will never please God. Even more, we must understand Paul's statement that all entreaties not joined with thanksgiving are wicked and vicious. For he speaks thus: "In all prayer," he says, "and supplication with thanksgiving let your petitions be made known to God" [Phil. 4:6]. For since many by peevishness, boredom, impatience, bitter grief, and fear are impelled to mumble when praying, he bids believers so to temper their emotions that while still waiting to obtain what they desire, they nonetheless cheerfully bless God. But if this connection ought to be in full force in things almost contrary, by a still holier bond God obligates us to sing his praises whenever he causes us to obtain our wishes.

Now even as we have taught that by Christ's intercession are consecrated our prayers, which would otherwise have been unclean, so the apostle, enjoining us to offer a sacrifice of praise through Christ [Heb. 13:15], warns us that our mouths are not clean enough to sing the praises of God's name until Christ's priesthood intercedes for us. . . .

The reason why Paul enjoins us both to pray and to give thanks without ceasing [1 Thess. 5:17–18; cf. 1 Tim. 2:1, 8] is, of course, that he wishes all men to lift up their desire to God, with all possible constancy, at all times, in all places, and in all affairs and transactions, to expect all things from him, and give him praise for all things, since he offers us unfailing reasons to praise and pray.

Necessity and danger of public prayer

This constancy in prayer, even though it has especially to do with one's own private prayers, still is also concerned somewhat with the public prayers of the church. Yet these can neither be constant nor ought they even to take place otherwise than according to the polity agreed upon by common consent among all. This I grant you. For this reason, certain hours, indifferent to God but necessary for men's convenience, are agreed upon and appointed to provide for the accommodation of all, and for everything to be done "decently and in order" in the church, according to Paul's statement [1 Cor. 14:40]. But this does not preclude each church from being both repeatedly stirred up to more frequent use of prayer and fired by a sharper zeal if it is alerted by some major need. There will be, moreover, toward the end, a place to speak of perseverance, which has close affinity with constancy.

Now these matters have nothing to do with the vain repetition that Christ willed to be forbidden to us [Matt. 6:7]. For Christ does not forbid us to persist in prayers, long, often, or with much feeling, but requires that we should not be confident in our ability to wrest something from God by beating upon his ears with a garrulous flow of talk, as if he could be persuaded as men are. For we know that hypocrites, because they do not reflect that they have to do with God, make the same pompous show in prayers as they would in a triumph. For that Pharisee who thanked God that he was not like other men [Luke 18:11] doubtless praised himself in men's eyes, as if he would from praying latch on to renown for holiness. Hence that vain repetition which for a similar reason is in vogue today in the papacy. While some pass the time in saying over and over the same little prayers, others vaunt themselves before the crowd with a great mass of words. Since this talkativeness childishly mocks God, it is no wonder that it is forbidden by the church in order that nothing shall resound there except what is earnest and comes forth from the depths of the heart.

Near and similar to this corrupt element is another, which Christ condemns at the same time: hypocrites, for the sake of show, pant after many witnesses, and would rather frequent the market place to pray than have their prayers miss the world's applause [Matt. 6:5]. But inasmuch as this goal of prayer has already been stated—namely, that hearts may be aroused and borne to God, whether to praise him or to beseech his help —from this we may understand that the essentials of prayer are set in the mind and heart, or rather that prayer itself is properly an emotion of the heart within, which is poured out and laid open before God, the searcher of hearts [cf. Rom. 8:27]. Accordingly, as has already been said, the Heavenly Teacher, when he willed to lay down the best rule for prayer, bade us enter into our bedroom and there, with door closed, pray to our Father in secret, that our Father, who is in secret, may hear us [Matt. 6:6]. For, when he has drawn us away from the example of hypocrites, who grasped after the favor of men by vain and ostentatious prayers, he at the same time adds something better: that is, to enter into our bedroom and there, with door closed, pray. By these words, as I understand them, he taught us to seek a retreat that would help us to descend into our heart with our whole thought and enter deeply within. He promises that God, whose temples our bodies ought to be, will be near to us in the affections of our hearts [cf. 2 Cor. 6:16].

For he did not mean to deny that it is fitting to pray in other places, but he shows that prayer is something secret, which is both principally lodged in the heart and requires a tranquillity far from all our teeming cares. The Lord himself also, therefore, with good reason, when he determined to devote himself more intensely to prayers, habitually withdrew to a quiet spot far away from the tumult of men; but he did so to

impress us with his example that we must not neglect
these helps, whereby our mind, too unsteady by itself,
more inclines to earnest application to prayer. In the
meantime, as he did not abstain from praying even in
the midst of a crowd if the occasion so presented itself,
so we should lift up clean hands in all places, where
there is need [1 Tim. 2:8]. Finally, we must consider that
whoever refused to pray in the holy assembly of the
godly knows not what it is to pray individually, or in
a secret spot, or at home. Again, he who neglects to
pray alone and in private, however unremittingly he
may frequent public assemblies, there contrives only
windy prayers, for he defers more to the opinion of
men than to the secret judgment of God.

Moreover, that the common prayers of the church
may not be held in contempt, God of old adorned them
with shining titles, especially when he called the temple the "house of prayer" [Isa. 56:7; Matt. 21:13]. For he
taught by this term that the chief part of his worship
lies in the office of prayer, and that the temple was set
up like a banner for believers so that they might, with
one consent, participate in it. A distinctive promise was
also added: "Praise waits for thee, O God, in Zion, and
to thee shall the vow be performed" [Ps. 65:1]. By these
words the prophet intimates that the prayers of the
church are never ineffectual, for God always furnishes
his people occasion for singing with joy. But even
though the shadows of the law have ceased, still there
is no doubt that the same promise pertains to us, since

God was pleased by this ceremony to foster the unity
of the faith among us. For not only has Christ sanc-
tioned this promise by his own mouth, but Paul holds
it to be universally in force.

*Not church buildings but we ourselves are temples of
God*

Now as God by his word ordains common prayers
for believers, so also ought there to be public temples
wherein these may be performed, in which those who
spurn fellowship with God's people in prayer have no
occasion to give the false excuse that they enter their
bedroom to obey the Lord's command. For he who
promises that he will do whatever two or three gathered together in his name may ask [Matt. 18:19–20] testifies that he does not despise prayers publicly made,
provided ostentation and chasing after paltry human
glory are banished, and there is present a sincere and
true affection that dwells in the secret place of the
heart.

If this is the lawful use of church buildings, as it
certainly is, we in turn must guard against either taking
them to be God's proper dwelling places, whence he
may more nearly incline his ear to us—as they began
to be regarded some centuries ago—or feigning for
them some secret holiness or other, which would render prayer more sacred before God. For since we ourselves are God's true temples, if we would call upon
God in his holy temple, we must pray within ourselves.

. . . For we have the commandment to call upon the Lord, without distinction of place, "in spirit and in truth" [John 4:23]. At God's command the Temple had indeed been dedicated of old for offering prayers and sacrificial victims, but at that time the truth lay hidden, figuratively represented under such shadows; now, having been expressed to us in living reality, it does not allow us to cleave to any material temple. And not even to the Jews was the Temple committed on the condition that they might shut up God's presence within its walls but in order that they might be trained to contemplate the likeness of the true Temple. Therefore, Isaiah and Stephen gravely rebuked those who thought God in any way dwells in temples made with hands [Isa. 66:1; Acts 7:48–49].

The use of singing and of the spoken language.
On speaking and singing in prayer
From this, moreover, it is fully evident that unless voice and song, if interposed in prayer, spring from deep feeling of heart, neither has any value or profit in the least with God. But they arouse his wrath against us if they come only from the tip of the lips and from the throat, seeing that this is to abuse his most holy name and to hold his majesty in derision. . . .

Yet we do not here condemn speaking and singing but rather strongly commend them, provided they are associated with the heart's affection. For thus do they exercise the mind in thinking of God and keep it attentive—unstable and variable as it is, and readily relaxed and diverted in different directions, unless it be supported by various helps. Moreover, since the glory of God ought, in a measure, to shine in the several parts of our bodies, it is especially fitting that the tongue has been assigned and destined for this task, both through singing and through speaking. For it was peculiarly created to tell and proclaim the praise of God. But the chief use of the tongue is in public prayers, which are offered in the assembly of believers, by which it comes about that with one common voice, and as it were, with the same mouth, we all glorify God together, worshiping him with one spirit and the same faith. And we do this openly, that all men mutually, each one from his brother, may receive the confession of faith and be invited and prompted by his example.

Church singing

It is evident that the practice of singing in church, to speak also of this in passing, is not only a very ancient one but also was in use among the apostles. This we may infer from Paul's words: "I will sing with the spirit and I will sing with the mind" [1 Cor. 14:15]. Likewise, Paul speaks to the Colossians: "Teaching and admonishing one another . . . in hymns, psalms, and spiritual songs, singing with thankfulness in your hearts to the Lord" [Col. 3:16]. For in the first passage he teaches that we should sing with voice and heart; in the second he commends spiritual songs, by which the godly may mutually edify one another.

Yet Augustine testifies that this practice was not universal when he states that the church of Milan first began to sing only under Ambrose; the occasion being that when Justina, the mother of Valentinian, was raging against the orthodox faith, the people were more constant in vigils than usual. Then the remaining Western churches followed Milan. For a little before he had said that this custom had come from the Eastern churches. He also indicates in the second book of his *Retractions* that the practice was taken up in Africa in his day. "A certain Hilary," he says, "an ex-tribune, attacked with malicious reproof, wherever he could, the custom, then just begun at Carthage, of singing hymns from the book of Psalms at the altar, either before the offering or when what had been offered was being distributed to the people. At the bidding of my brethren, I answered him."

And surely, if the singing be tempered to that gravity which is fitting in the sight of God and the angels, it both lends dignity and grace to sacred actions and has the greatest value in kindling our hearts to a true zeal and eagerness to pray. Yet we should be very careful that our ears be not more attentive to the melody than our minds to the spiritual meaning of the words. Augustine also admits in another place that he was so disturbed by this danger that he sometimes wished to see established the custom observed by Athanasius, who ordered the reader to use so little inflection of the voice that he would sound more like a speaker than a singer. But when he recalled how much benefit singing had brought him, he inclined to the other side. Therefore, when this moderation is maintained, it is without any doubt a most holy and salutary practice. On the other hand, such songs as have been composed only for sweetness and delight of the ear are unbecoming to the majesty of the church and cannot but displease God in the highest degree.

Prayer should be in the language of the people

From this also it plainly appears that public prayers must be couched not in Greek among the Latins, nor in Latin among the French or English, as has heretofore been the custom, but in the language of the people, which can be generally understood by the whole assembly. For this ought to be done for the edification of the whole church, which receives no benefit whatever from a sound not understood. Those who have no regard for either love or kindliness ought at least to have been moved a little by the authority of Paul, whose words are perfectly clear. "If you bless with the spirit," he says, "how can he who occupies the place of the unlearned respond to your blessing with 'Amen,' since he is ignorant of what you are saying? For you indeed give thanks, but the other is not edified" [1 Cor. 14:16–17]. . . .

But for us Paul prescribes otherwise what is to be

done. "What am I to do?" he says, "I will pray with the spirit, I will pray with the mind also: I will sing with the spirit and I will sing with the mind also" [1 Cor. 14:15]. By the word "spirit" he means the singular gift of tongues, which some, though endowed therewith, abused, since they cut it off from the mind, that is, the understanding. However, we must unquestionably feel that, either in public prayer or in private, the tongue without the mind must be highly displeasing to God. Besides, the mind ought to be kindled with an ardor of thought so as far to surpass all that the tongue can express by speaking.

Lastly, we should hold that the tongue is not even necessary for private prayer, except insofar as either the inner feeling has insufficient power to arouse itself or as it is so vehemently aroused that it carries with it the action of the tongue. For even though the best prayers are sometimes unspoken, it often happens in practice that, when feelings of mind are aroused, unostentatiously the tongue breaks forth into speech, and the other members into gesture. From this obviously arose that uncertain murmur of Hannah's [1 Sam. 1:13], something similar to which all the saints continually experience when they burst forth into broken and fragmentary speech.

As for the bodily gestures customarily observed in praying, such as kneeling and uncovering the head, they are exercises whereby we try to rise to a greater reverence for God. . . .

The Lord's Prayer.

The Lord's Prayer as a binding rule

We have everything we ought, or are at all able, to seek of God, set forth in this form and, as it were, rule for prayer handed down by our best Master, Christ, whom the Father has appointed our teacher and to whom alone he would have us hearken [Matt. 17:5]. For he both has always been the eternal Wisdom of God [Isa. 11:2] and, made man, has been given to men, the angel of great counsel [Isa. 9:6, conflated with ch. 28:29 and Jer. 32:19].

And this prayer is in all respects so perfect that any extraneous or alien thing added to it, which cannot be related to it, is impious and unworthy to be approved by God. For in this summary he has set forth what is worthy of him, acceptable to him, necessary for us—in effect, what he would willingly grant. . . .

The Lord's Prayer does not bind us to its form of words but to its content

We would not have it understood that we are so bound by this form of prayer that we are not allowed to change it in either word or syllable. For here and there in Scripture one reads many prayers, far different from it in words, yet composed by the same Spirit, the use of which is very profitable to us. Many prayers are repeatedly suggested to believers by the same Spirit, which bear little similarity in wording. In so teaching, we mean only this: that no man should ask for, expect, or demand, anything at all except what is included, by way of summary, in this prayer; and though the words may be utterly different, yet the sense ought not to vary. Thus all prayers contained in Scripture, and those which come forth from godly breasts, are certainly to be referred to it. Truly, no other can ever be found that equals this in perfection, much less surpasses it. Here nothing is left out that ought to be thought of in the praises of God, nothing that ought to come into man's mind for his own welfare. And, indeed, it is so precisely framed that hope of attempting anything better is rightly taken away from all men. To sum up, let us remember that this is the teaching of Divine Wisdom, teaching what it willed and willing what was needful.

Special times of prayer and undiscouraged perseverance in it.

Prayer at regular times

But, although it has already been stated above that, lifting up our hearts, we should ever aspire to God and pray without ceasing, still, since our weakness is such that it has to be supported by many aids, and our sluggishness such that it needs to be goaded, it is fitting each one of us should set apart certain hours for this exercise. Those hours should not pass without prayer, and during them all the devotion of the heart should be completely engaged in it. These are: when we arise in the morning, before we begin daily work, when we sit down to a meal, when by God's blessing we have eaten, when we are getting ready to retire.

But this must not be any superstitious observance of hours, whereby, as if paying our debt to God, we imagine ourselves paid up for the remaining hours. Rather, it must be a tutelage for our weakness, which should be thus exercised and repeatedly stimulated. We must take particular care that, whenever we either are pressed or see others pressed by any adversity, we hasten back to God, not with swift feet but with eager hearts. Also, that we should not let our prosperity or that of others go unnoticed, failing to testify, by praise and thanksgiving, that we recognize God's hand therein.

Lastly, in all prayer we ought carefully to observe that our intention is not to bind God to particular circumstances, or to prescribe at what time, in what place, or in what way he is to do anything. Accordingly, in this prayer we are taught not to make any law for him, or impose any condition upon him, but to leave to his decision to do what he is to do, in what way, at what time, and in what place it seems good to him. Therefore, before we make any prayer for ourselves, we pray that his will be done [Matt. 6:10]. By these words we subject our will to his in order that, restrained as by a bridle, it may not presume to control God but may make him the arbiter and director of all its entreaties.

Institutes III. 20

PRAYERS

My God, my Father and Preserver, who of thy goodness hast watched over me during the past night, and brought me to this day, grant also that I may spend it wholly in the worship and service of thy most holy deity. Let me not think, or say, or do a single thing which tends not to thy service and submission to thy will, that thus all my actions may aim at thy glory and the salvation of my brethren, while they are taught by my example to serve thee. And as thou art giving light to this world for the purposes of external life by the rays of the sun, so enlighten my mind by the effulgence of thy Spirit, that he may guide me in the way of thy righteousness. To whatever purpose I apply my mind, may the end which I ever propose to myself be thy honor and service. May I expect all happiness from thy grace and goodness only. Let me not attempt anything whatever that is not pleasing to thee.

Grant also, that while I labor for the maintenance of this life, and care for the things which pertain to food and raiment, I may raise my mind above them to the blessed and heavenly life which thou hast promised to thy children. Be pleased also, in manifesting thyself to me as the protector of my soul as well as my body, to strengthen and fortify me against all the assaults of the devil, and deliver me from all the dangers which continually beset us in this life. But seeing it is a small thing to have begun, unless I also persevere, I therefore entreat of thee, O Lord, not only to be my guide and director for this day, but to keep me under thy protection to the very end of life, that thus my whole course may be performed under thy superintendence. As I ought to make progress, do thou add daily more and more to the gifts of thy grace until I wholly adhere to thy Son Jesus Christ, whom we justly regard as the true Sun, shining constantly in our minds. In order to my obtaining of thee these great and manifold blessings, forget, and out of thy infinite mercy, forgive my offenses, as thou hast promised that thou wilt do to those who call upon thee in sincerity. Amen.

Let me hear in the morning of thy steadfast love, for in thee I put my trust. Teach me the way I should go, for to thee I lift up my soul. Deliver me, O Lord, from my enemies! I have fled to thee for refuge! Teach me to do thy will, for thou art my God! Let thy good spirit lead me on a level path! [Ps. 143:8–10]

BEFORE GOING TO WORK

Our good God, Father and Savior, since thou hast commanded us to work in order to meet our needs, sanctify our labor so that thy blessing extends even to us, without which no one can ever prosper well. Let such favor attend us as a witness of thy goodness and help, making us aware through it of the fatherly care thou hast for us. Also, Lord, be pleased to assist us through thy Holy Spirit to the end that we are able faithfully to fulfill our calling without any deceit or fraud, that we regard ourselves as following thy law rather than fulfilling our desire to enrich ourselves. Nevertheless, let it please thee to prosper our labor. Give thou also to us a good heart to supply those who are poor, maintaining us in all humility to the end that we may never exalt ourselves over those who have not received such largesse from your liberality. Now if thou should call us into greater poverty or need than we humanly desire, let us not sink into defiance but rather let us wait patiently for thee to replenish us not only with temporal grace but also with thy spiritual grace to the end that we may always have more ample cause and occasion to thank thee and to rest entirely upon thy goodness. Grant this to us, Father of all mercy, through Jesus Christ, your Son, our Savior. Amen.

How can a young man keep his way pure? By guarding it according to thy word. With my whole heart I seek thee; let me not wander from thy commandments! [Ps. 119:9–10]

O Lord, who art the fountain of all wisdom and learning, since thou of thy special goodness hast granted that my youth is instructed in good arts which may assist me to honest and holy living, grant also, by enlightening my mind, which otherwise labors under blindness, that I may be fit to acquire knowledge; strengthen my memory faithfully to retain what I may have learned: and govern my heart, that I may be willing and even eager to profit, lest the opportunity which thou now givest me be lost through my sluggishness. Be pleased therefore to infuse thy Spirit into me, the Spirit of understanding, of truth, judgment, and prudence, lest my study be without success, and the labor of my teacher be in vain.

In whatever kind of study I engage, enable me to remember to keep its proper end in view, namely, to know thee in Christ Jesus thy Son; and may every thing that I learn assist me to observe the right rule of godliness. And seeing thou promisest that thou wilt bestow wisdom on babes, and such as are humble, and the knowledge of thyself on the upright in heart, while thou declarest that thou wilt cast down the wicked and the proud, so that they will fade away in their ways, I entreat that thou wouldst be pleased to turn me to true humility, that thus I may show myself teachable and obedient first of all to thyself, and then to those also who by thy authority are placed over me. Be pleased at the same time to root out all vicious desires from my heart, and inspire it with an earnest desire of seeking thee. Finally, let the only end at which I aim be so to qualify myself in early life, that when I grow up I may serve thee in whatever station thou mayest assign me. Amen.

The friendship of the Lord is for those who fear him, and he makes known to them his covenant. [Ps. 25:14]

BLESSING AT TABLE

These all look to thee, to give them their food in due season. When thou givest to them, they gather it up; when thou openest thy hand, they are filled with good things. [Ps. 104:27–28]

O Lord, in whom is the source and inexhaustible fountain of all good things, pour out thy blessing upon us, and sanctify to our use the meat and drink which are the gifts of thy kindness toward us, that we, using them soberly and frugally as thou enjoinest, may eat with a pure conscience. Grant, also, that we may always both with true heartfelt gratitude acknowledge, and with our lips proclaim thee our Father and the giver of all good, and, while enjoying bodily nourishment, aspire with special longing of heart after the bread of thy doctrine, by which our souls may be nourished in the hope of eternal life, through Christ Jesus our Lord. Amen.

Man does not live by bread alone, but by everything that proceeds out of the mouth of the Lord. [Deut. 8:3]

THANKSGIVING AFTER A MEAL

Praise the Lord, all nations! Extol him, all peoples! For great is his steadfast love toward us: and the faithfulness of the Lord endures forever. Praise the Lord. [Ps. 117:1–2]

We give thanks, O God and Father, for the many mercies which thou of thy infinite goodness art constantly bestowing upon us; both in that by supplying all the helps which we need to sustain the present life, thou showest that thou hast a care even of our bodies, and more especially in that thou hast deigned to beget us again to the hope of the better life which thou hast revealed to us by thy holy gospel. And we beseech thee not to allow our minds to be chained down to earthly thoughts and cares, as if they were buried in our bodies. Rather cause that we may stand with eyes upraised in expectation of thy Son Jesus Christ, till he appear from heaven for our redemption and salvation. Amen.

AT NIGHT ON GOING TO SLEEP

O Lord God, who hast given man the night for rest, as thou hast created the day in which he may employ himself in labor, grant, I pray, that my body may so rest during this night that my mind cease not to be awake to thee, nor my heart faint or be overcome with torpor, preventing it from adhering steadfastly to the love of thee. While laying aside my cares to relax and relieve my mind, may I not, in the meanwhile, forget thee, nor may the remembrance of thy goodness and grace, which ought always to be deeply engraven on my mind, escape my memory. In like manner, also, as the body rests may my conscience enjoy rest. Grant, moreover, that in taking sleep I may not give indulgence to the flesh, but only allow myself as much as the weakness of this natural state requires, to my being enabled thereafter to be more alert in thy service. Be pleased to keep me so chaste and unpolluted, not less in mind than in body, and safe from all dangers, that my sleep itself may turn to the glory of thy name. But since this day has not passed away without my having in many ways offended thee through my proneness to evil, in like manner as all things are now covered by the darkness of the night, so let every thing that is sinful in me lie buried in thy mercy. Hear me, O God, Father and Preserver, through Jesus Christ thy Son. Amen.

4

Election: The Ground and Source of the Christian Life

A SERMON ON EPHESIANS 1:3–4

We have already seen how St. Paul exhorts us to praise and bless God because he has blessed us, and that not after an earthly manner but after a spiritual manner, so that we should content ourselves with God's showing of his fatherly goodness and love toward us in opening the gate of the kingdom of heaven to us by hope. Although we are subject to much misery in this world, yet there is good reason for us to content ourselves with God's choosing of us after that fashion and with his calling of us to himself, for it is witnessed to us by the gospel that he is our Father [Matt. 6:9; Luke 11:2] inasmuch as he has joined us to our Lord Jesus Christ as members to their Head.

And now St. Paul brings us to the origin and source, or rather to the principal cause that moved God to take us into his favor. For it is not enough that God has revealed the treasures of his goodness and mercy to us to draw us to the hope of the heavenly life by the gospel —and yet that is very much. For had not St. Paul added that which we see now, it might have been surmised that God's grace is common to all men and that he offers it and presents it to all without exception, and, consequently, that it is in every man's power to receive it according to his own free will, by which means there would be some merit in us. For if there were no distinction between men except that some receive God's grace and others refuse it, what could be said but that God has shown himself liberal to all mankind? But they that are partakers of the grace of our Lord Jesus Christ attain to it by faith. And so you see what might be judged of it. But St. Paul, to exclude all merit on man's part and to show that all comes from God's pure goodness and grace, says that he has blessed us according to his election of us beforehand. As if he should say that to exalt God's grace as becomes us, we must look upon the diversity that is found among men. For the gospel is preached to some, and others do not know what it is but are utterly shut out from it, as if God should make it rain in one quarter and allow another quarter to remain very dry.

Now if it is demanded why God pities the one part and forsakes and leaves and abandons the other, there is no other answer but that it so pleases him. Upon the preaching of the gospel in a place, some will be affected with lively faith in their hearts and others will go away as they came without benefiting at all, or else they harden themselves against God and betray the stubbornness that was hidden in them before. What is the reason for this difference? Even this, that God directs the one sort by his Holy Spirit and leaves the other sort in their natural corruption.

You see then that the thing in which God's goodness shines forth most to us, is that by the preaching of the gospel to us we have, as it were, a token that he has pitied us, loves us, calls us and allures us to him. But when the doctrine preached to us is received by us with heart and affection, that is yet a further and more special token by which we perceive that God intends to be our Father and has adopted us to be his children. Not without reason, then, St. Paul says in this passage that we are blessed by God even according to his election of us beforehand. For it is not that we have come to him; it is not that we have sought him. But the saying of the prophet Isaiah [65:1] must be fulfilled in every respect, namely, that God shows himself to such as did not seek him, and that such as were far off see him near at hand, and he says to them, "Here I am, here I am. Although you have despised me, yet I vouchsafe to come to you because I have a care of your salvation." Thus we see what St. Paul was aiming at in this passage.

In short, we have to note here that we shall never know where our salvation comes from till we have lifted up our minds to God's eternal counsel by which he has chosen whom he pleased and left the remainder in their confusion and ruin. Now then it is no marvel that some men think this doctrine to be strange and hard, for it does not fit in at all with man's natural understanding. If a man asks of the philosophers, they will always tell him that God loves such as are worthy of it, and that, since virtue pleases him, he also marks out such as are given that way to claim them for his people. You see then that, after our own imagination, we shall judge that God puts no other difference between men, in loving some and in hating others, than each man's own worthiness and deserving. But, at the same time, let us also remember that in our own understanding there is nothing but vanity and that we must not measure God by our own yardstick, and that it is too excessive a presumption to impose law upon God so that it would not be lawful for him to do anything but that which we could conceive and which might seem just in our eyes. The matter here, therefore, concerns the reverencing of God's secrets which are incomprehensible to us, and unless we do so, we shall never taste the principles of faith. For we know that our wisdom ought always to begin with humility, and this humility imports that we must not come weighing God's judgments in our own balances or take it upon ourselves to be judges and arbiters of them. We must be sober because of the smallness of our minds, and since we are gross and dull, we must magnify God and say, as we are taught by the holy Scripture [Ps. 36:6], Lord, thy counsels are as a great deep, and no man is able to give an account of them.

You see then that the reason why some men find this doctrine hard and irksome is because they are too much wedded to their own opinion and cannot submit themselves to God's wisdom, to receive his sayings soberly and modestly. And truly we ought to take warning from what St. Paul says, namely, that the natural man does not understand God's secrets but regards them as stark foolishness [1 Cor. 2:14]. And why? Because we are not his counselors but must have things revealed to us by his Holy Spirit, or else we shall never know them, and we must have them in such measure as he gives them to us.

St. Paul speaks here of the things we know by experience, namely, that we are God's children, that he governs us by his Holy Spirit, that he comforts us in our miseries and that he strengthens us through patience. We should not conceive any of all these things unless we were enlightened by his Holy Spirit. How then shall we understand that which is much higher, namely, that God elected us before the creation of the world? Since the matter stands thus, let us learn to put away all that we conceive in our own brain and put it under foot, and let us be ready to receive whatever God says to us, casting away our own judgment and assuring ourselves that we cannot bring anything from our side but utter stupidity. Thus you see what we have to bear in mind.

And, in fact, we see how St. Paul exhorts us to come to the same point. "Who art thou, O man (he says), who contends against thy God?" [Rom. 9:20]. After he had set down many replies we are accustomed to make, he says, "O man." By the word "man" he meant to make us perceive our own frailty, for we are but worms of earth and rottenness [Ps. 103:14]. Now then, what audacity it is to open our mouths to reply against God. Is it not a perverting of the whole order of nature? Is it in our power to pluck the sun out of the sky, or to take the moon between our teeth, as they say? Much less is it lawful for us to contend with God and to advance reasons for controlling his judgments which we cannot comprehend.

There are those who will grant this doctrine of predestination, which St. Paul treats here, to be true, for they dare not contradict the Holy Spirit, yet they would it were buried so that it might never be spoken of. But they merely show themselves to be nothing but fools in controlling the Holy Spirit who spoke it by the prophets and apostles, and even by the mouth of God's only Son. For when our Lord intends to assure us of our salvation, he brings us back to this eternal election; and similarly when he intends to magnify the gift of faith, the one in the tenth chapter of John and the other in the sixth. And therefore that kind of people come too late to put God to silence and to efface from the holy Scripture the things which are shown there. For the whole Scripture is profitable [2 Tim. 3:16]. St. Paul said that of the Law and the Prophets. Therefore we may also conclude that there is nothing superfluous in the gospel, nor anything which serves no good purpose and by which we may not be edified both in faith and in the fear of God. . . .

But there are yet two more reasons which show that

this doctrine must of necessity be preached, and that we reap such great profit from it that it had been much better if we had never been born than be ignorant of what St. Paul shows here. For there are two things at which we must chiefly aim and to which it is fitting for us to apply all our studies and endeavours, and they are the very sum of all the things God teaches us by the holy Scripture. The one is the magnifying of God as he deserves, and the other is the assurance of our salvation, so that we may call on him as our Father with full liberty [Rom. 8:15]. If we do not have these two things, woe to us, for there is neither faith nor religion in us. We may talk well of God, but it will be but falsehood.

With regard to the first point, I have told you already that God's grace is not sufficiently known but by setting God's election, as it were, before our eyes. For suppose God draws all men alike, and that such as wish to obtain salvation must come of their own free will and self-moving. If it be so, then it is certain that we deserve to be received at God's hand, and that he should handle every man according to his deserts. But how shall God's goodness be magnified? Simply in this way, that he goes before us by his pure bounty and loves us despite all, without finding either in our persons or in our works any reason why he should love us. If this is true, then there must needs be election: God takes the one sort because he thinks it good to do so, and leaves the other. Thus you see it is a most certain point that God's glory does not appear and shine forth as is fitting, unless it be known that he sheds forth his goodness and love where it pleases him.

I said just now that the preaching of his Word is a singular benefit to us. And that is the reason why it is said so often in the Law and the Prophets that God has not dealt with any other nation as he dealt with the line of Abraham, in that he vouchsafed to choose and adopt them, to which the law gave sure testimony. So then the children of Israel were exhorted to praise God because he had vouchsafed to give them his law [Deut. 4:7], and, in the meanwhile, had let the poor Gentiles alone as people that did not belong to him after the same fashion. But it is yet a far greater and more special privilege when he makes us profit by that Word. For it is certain that our ears might be assailed daily with the things that should be told us and that we would never be the better for it, until God speaks to us by his Holy Spirit within us.

In this matter, then, God shows a double grace. The one is when he raises up men to preach the gospel to us, for no man is meet and sufficient to do it of himself. It is therefore necessary that God should send those who call us to him and offer us the hope of salvation. But yet, for all that, let us note well that we cannot believe unless God reveals himself to us by his Holy Spirit and speaks to our hearts by the Holy Spirit, in addition to speaking to our ears by the mouth of man. And that is the reason why the prophet Isaiah says, "Who hath believed our doctrine, and to whom is the arm of the Lord revealed?" [Isa. 53:1]. He shows that there is no faith in the world till God has worked in men's minds and hearts by the power of his Holy Spirit. And for the very same reason also our Lord Jesus Christ says that no man comes to him except he be drawn by the Father; but whoever has learned of my Father (he says), the same submits himself to me [John 6:44]. In a word, we see clearly that God shows himself merciful to us when he vouchsafes to enlighten us by his Holy Spirit in order that we might be drawn to the faith of his gospel.

If this was done commonly and to all men without distinction, we should still have reason to magnify God. But now, when we see that some are hardened and others fickle, and that some go their ways without receiving any profit from what they have heard, and that others are altogether stupid, it is certain that it makes God's grace more apparent to us, even as it is said by St. Luke that, at St. Paul's preaching, as many believed as were ordained to salvation [Acts 13:48]. Truly a multitude of people heard St. Paul's sermon, and, beyond all doubt, he on his side had such grace that it ought to have moved even the very stones. Nevertheless, despite this, a great many continued in their unbelief and stubbornness; others believed.

Now St. Luke says plainly that it was not that some were more clever than others, or that there was more inclination to virtue in them than in others, but that God had specially ordained them to salvation. In a word, therefore, we see that all man's merits must cease and be laid underfoot, or else God will not have the praise he deserves. Furthermore, we must understand that faith comes not of ourselves, for if it did, there would be some merit in our works. It is true that by faith we confess that there is nothing but wretchedness in us, that we are damned and accursed, and that we do not bring anything with us but only an acknowledgment of our sins. But, even so, our faith would qualify as a thing of merit if we had it through our own initiative. We must therefore conclude that it is impossible for men to believe, unless it is given them from above.

And surely St. Paul here declares something well worth observing when he says "Blessed be God." And for what reason? Even for so enriching us in Jesus Christ that our life is happy and blessed. And afterwards he adds, "according to his election of us." Is not faith comprehended among the spiritual riches of which St. Paul makes mention? Indeed, and (what is more) it is the chief of them. For it is by faith that we receive the Holy Spirit; it is by faith that we become patient in our adversities; it is by faith that we become obedient to God; it is by faith that we are sanctified to his service. In short, faith continues always chief of all the spiritual benefits that God bestows upon us.

Now let us well remember St. Paul's order. He says that God has given us faith as well as any of the rest, according to his election of us. We see then that faith depends upon God's election, or else we must make St. Paul a liar. And so, with regard to the first point, you see that all who cannot suffer having predestination plainly and openly spoken of, are deadly enemies of

God's grace and would make it obscure to the utmost of their power. For (as I said before) to hide it is to overthrow all religion.

The second point is the assurance of our salvation. [Some] say that we must doubt it and that we can come to God only with a hope that he will receive us; but to assure ourselves of it—that we ought not to do, for that would be too great a presumption. But when we pray to God, we must call him Father, at least if we are the scholars of our Lord Jesus Christ, for he has taught us to do so. Now, is it at a venture that we call him Father, or are we sure of it in ourselves that he is our Father? If not, then there would be nothing but hypocrisy in our prayers, and the first word that we utter would be a lie. . . . The Scripture shows that to pray to God rightly, we must have belief in Jesus Christ, which gives us confidence, and upon that confidence we by and by conceive boldness. Be that as it may, we must not be hesitant nor yet doubt, but we must be thoroughly resolved and persuaded in ourselves that God counts us as his children. And how may that be but by embracing his mercy through faith, as he offers it to us in his gospel, and by assuring ourselves also that we are grounded in his eternal election? For if our faith should depend upon ourselves, surely it would soon slip from us; and it might be shaken off, if it were not maintained from above. And although we are kept or preserved by faith, as St. Peter says [1 Pet. 1:5], yet it is God who keeps us. If, then, our faith were not grounded in God's eternal election, it is certain that

Satan might pluck it from us every minute. Though today we were the most steadfast in the world, yet we might fail tomorrow. But our Lord Jesus shows us the remedy to strengthen us against all temptations in that he says: You do not come to me of yourselves, but the heavenly Father brings you to me; and since I have taken you into my keeping, be no more afraid, for I acknowledge you as the inheritance of God my Father, and he that has given me charge of you and put you into my hand is stronger than all [John 10:28–29]. We see, then, that besides setting forth God's glory, our salvation also is assured by God's eternal predestination, which ought to be sufficient reason to move us to consider what St. Paul says of it in this place.

It is true (as I have mentioned already) that many men cavil when they hear that God has elected those as it seemed good to him and rejected all the rest. For we see that it is the smaller portion that come to God; and why then has he rejected the rest? Really, it is rather like saying that the will of God should not suffice for our rule. We ought to note, first, that God is not bound at all to any person. For if we once held that principle, that he owes us the least thing in the world, then we call in question his law. But since he on his side has no obligation towards us, but that we owe everything to him while he owes nothing to us, let us see now what we shall gain by all our contending. For if we aim at compelling God to deal alike with all men, he would have less liberty than mortal creatures. If a man is rich, he may do what he likes with his own goods. If he makes a gift to someone, is it reason that he should be sued at the law for it, and that every man should demand the same sum from him? Again, a man wishes to promote someone whom he loves. Now if all poor people should come and require him to do as much for them as a matter of obligation, would it not be ridiculous? Why, a man may adopt the most distant stranger in the world to be his child and heir, and he is free to do so. And mark, God is liberal to all men, for he makes his sun to shine upon both good and bad [Matt. 5:45]. He reserves only a certain number of men on whom to bestow the privilege of adopting them as his children. What shall we now gain by murmuring against him? If any man says that then he would seem to be a respecter of persons, it is not so [Col. 3:25]. For he does not elect the rich and pass over the poor; he does not choose noble men and gentlemen rather than men of no account and low degree [1 Cor. 1:26]. And therefore it cannot be said that there is any respecting of persons before God, for in choosing those that are unworthy he has respect to his own pure goodness alone. Nor does he consider whether one is more worthy than another, but he takes whom he pleases.

What more could we wish? It is good reason, then, that we should hold ourselves contented with God's will and check ourselves and leave him to choose whom he pleases, because his will is the sovereign standard of all equity and right. And so you see the mouths of all the world stopped [Rom. 3:19]. And although the wicked and profane murmur and find fault, or even blaspheme, yet God is mighty enough to maintain his own righteousness and infinite wisdom, and when they have jabbered their fill, they are sure to be confounded in the end. For our part we see what St. Paul says here. For it is no obscure doctrine when he says that God has blessed us. Truly, inasmuch as he has enlightened us with the faith of the gospel by his Holy Spirit and made us partakers of the grace of our Lord Jesus Christ, even thereby (he says) he has shown that he had elected us before the creation of the world. And therefore let us understand that to magnify God's grace aright, we must (as I said before) come to this fountain and original cause, that is to say, to election.

Now we have to proceed further, for in order the better to exclude all respect and worthiness which men might pretend, since we are inclined always to attribute something to ourselves and cannot bear to be brought to nothing, he says, "before the creation of the world." So then, since through such thinking we imagine ourselves to have that which we do not have, it was essential that St. Paul should here beat down all such ridiculous folly. . . .

How then do we come to God? How do we obey him? How do we have a quiet mind that yields itself in accordance with faith? All these things come from him, and so it follows that he must do all himself. Wherefore let us observe that in saying that God elected us before the creation of the world, St. Paul presupposes that which is true, namely, that God could not see anything in us save the evil that was there, for

there was not one drop of goodness for him to find. So
then, seeing he has elected us, regard it as a very clear
token of his free grace. And for the same reason, in the
ninth chapter to the Romans, where he speaks of the
twins Jacob and Esau at such time as they were still in
their mother's womb before they had done either good
or evil, it is said that the elder should serve the younger
so that all should come from the side of him who called
them, and not from the side of their works [Rom.
9:11–12].

We see then how St. Paul shows there at greater
length that which he here touches on briefly, that is to
say, that since God chose us before the creation of the
world, he thereby shows sufficiently that one man is
not more worthy or excellent than another; that he did
not have respect to worthiness. Therefore, seeing that
the distinguishing between Jacob and Esau was before
they had done either good or evil, it did not come of
the works but of the caller. All praise, then, must be
yielded to God and nothing at all be reserved to man.
And so you see yet once again what we have to note
here when St. Paul says that we were elected before the
creation of the world.

He confirms the thing in better fashion still by saying that the same was done in Jesus Christ. If we had
been elected in ourselves it might be said that God had
found in us some secret virtue unknown to men. But
seeing that he has elected us outside of ourselves, that
is to say, loved us outside of ourselves, what shall we
reply to that? If I do a man good, it is because I love

him. And if the cause of my love is sought, it will be because we are alike in character, or else for some other good reason. But we must not imagine anything similar to this in God. And also it is expressly told us here, for St. Paul says that we have been elected in Jesus Christ. Did God, then, have an eye to us when he vouchsafed to love us? No! No! For then he would have utterly abhorred us. It is true that in regarding our miseries he had pity and compassion on us to relieve us, but that was because he had already loved us in our Lord Jesus Christ. God, then, must have had before him his pattern and mirror in which to see us, that is to say, he must have first looked on our Lord Jesus Christ before he could choose us and call us.

And so, to be brief, after St. Paul had showed that we could not bring anything to God, but that he acted beforehand of his own free grace in electing us before the creation of the world, he adds an even more certain proof, namely, that he did it in our Lord Jesus Christ, who is, as it were, the true register. For God's vouchsafing to elect us, that is to say, his vouchsafing to do it from all eternity, was, as it were, a registering of us in writing. And the holy Scripture calls God's election the book of life. As I said before, Jesus Christ serves as a register. It is in him that we are written down and acknowledged by God as his children. Seeing, then, that God had an eye to us in the person of Jesus Christ, it follows that he did not find anything in us which we might lay before him to cause him to elect us. This, in sum, is what we must always remember.

It follows next that it is "in order that we should be

pure and unblameable before God in love." This word "love" may be referred to God, as if it were said that we shall find no other reason why God vouchsafed to take us for his children, but only his own free love. Or else (as seems very likely) St. Paul shows us here what the true soundness and perfection of the faithful is, namely, to walk in all righteousness before God. We cannot expound the whole now, but it will suffice to tell briefly what St. Paul had in view. For he shows here that although God's election is free and beats down and annihilates all the worthiness, works and virtues of men, nevertheless it does not provide us with license to do evil and to lead a disordered life, or to run amok, but rather it serves to withdraw us from the evil in which we were plunged. For, by nature, we can do nothing else but provoke God's wrath; wickedness will always reign in us; and we are held down under the bonds and tyranny of Satan. God, therefore, must work and change us, for all goodness comes from his election, says St. Paul.

You see, then, that that to which he meant to bring the faithful was to make them know that just as God elected them of his own free grace, so he does not give them leave to yield themselves to all wickedness, but intends to keep and preserve them undefiled to himself. For God's electing of us and, with that, his calling of us to holiness are things joined inseparably together, even as St. Paul says in another passage, that we are not called to uncleanness and filthiness, but to be dedicated to God in all piety and holiness [I Thess. 4:7].

Now, since we cannot expound the whole at this

time, let us seek to profit from this doctrine. And seeing we are now about to prepare ourselves to receive the supper of our Lord Jesus Christ, which is a pledge to us of our election, as well as the hope of our salvation and of all the spiritual benefits that come forth from this source and fountain of God's free love, let us know that there he displays his riches to us not so that we should abuse them, but rather with the purpose of being glorified for them at our hands, not only with our mouths but also with our whole life. And since we hold all things of him, let us also learn to be his and to give ourselves up to his obedience, that he may enjoy us peaceably. And let us always aim at this mark, namely, to get a sure approbation that he takes and owns us for his children, by bearing his marks and by showing in every deed that we are truly governed by his Holy Spirit in calling upon him as our Father. Thus you see, in effect, what we have to observe in this passage till the rest follows.

Now let us fall down before the majesty of our good God with acknowledgment of our faults, praying him to make us feel them in such a way that we may continually profit in his fear, and be strengthened more and more in the same; and, in the meanwhile, so to bear with our weaknesses that we may always enjoy his grace even till he has set us in possession of all things at such time as he shall have put away our sins and blotted them out completely for our Lord Jesus Christ's sake.

5

Life in the Church

The necessity of the church

. . . . It is by the faith in the gospel that Christ becomes ours and we are made partakers of the salvation and eternal blessedness brought by him. Since, however, in our ignorance and sloth (to which I add fickleness of disposition) we need outward helps to beget and increase faith within us, and advance it to its goal, God has also added these aids that he may provide for our weakness. And in order that the preaching of the gospel might flourish, he deposited this treasure in the church. He instituted "pastors and teachers" [Eph. 4:11] through whose lips he might teach his own; he furnished them with authority; finally, he omitted nothing that might make for holy agreement of faith and for right order. First of all, he instituted sacraments, which we who have experienced them feel to be highly useful aids to foster and strengthen faith. Shut up as we are in the prison house of our flesh, we have not yet attained angelic rank. God, therefore, in his wonderful providence accommodating himself to our capacity, has prescribed a way for us, though still far off, to draw near to him. . . .

I shall start, then, with the church, into whose bosom God is pleased to gather his sons, not only that they may be nourished by her help and ministry as long as they are infants and children, but also that they may be guided by her motherly care until they mature and at last reach the goal of faith. "For what God has joined together, it is not lawful to put asunder" [Mark 10:9], so that, for those to whom he is Father the church may also be Mother. And this was so not only under the law but also after Christ's coming, as Paul testifies when he teaches that we are the children of the new and heavenly Jerusalem [Gal. 4:26]. . . .

The church is called "catholic," or "universal," because there could not be two or three churches unless Christ be torn asunder [cf. 1 Cor. 1:13]—which cannot happen! But all the elect are so united in Christ [cf. Eph. 1:22–23] that as they are dependent on one Head, they also grow together into one body, being joined and knit together [cf. Eph. 4:16] as are the limbs of a body [Rom. 12:5; 1 Cor. 10:17; 12:12, 27]. They are made truly one since they live together in one faith, hope, and love, and in the same Spirit of God. For they have been called not only into the same inheritance of eternal life but also to participate in one God and Christ [Eph. 5:30]. Although the melancholy desolation which confronts us on every side may cry that no remnant of the church is left, let us know that Christ's death is fruitful, and that God miraculously keeps his church as in hiding places. So it was said to Elijah, "I have kept for myself seven thousand men who have not bowed the knee before Baal" [1 Kings 19:18].

"The communion of saints"

This article of the Creed also applies to some extent to the outward church, in that each of us should keep in brotherly agreement with all God's children, should yield to the church the authority it deserves, in short, should act as one of the flock. Accordingly, "the communion of saints" is added. This clause, though generally omitted by the ancients, ought not to be overlooked, for it very well expresses what the church is. It is as if one said that the saints are gathered into the society of Christ on the principle that whatever benefits God confers upon them, they should in turn share with one another. This does not, however, rule out diversity of graces, inasmuch as we know the gifts of the Spirit are variously distributed. Nor is civil order disturbed, which allows each individual to own his private possessions, since it is necessary to keep peace among men that the ownership of property should be distinct and personal among them. But a community is affirmed, such as Luke describes, in which the heart and soul of the multitude of believers are one [Acts 4:32]; and such as Paul has in mind when he urges the Ephesians to be "one body and one Spirit, just as" they "were called in one hope" [Eph. 4:4]. If truly convinced that God is the common Father of all and Christ the common Head, being united in brotherly love, they cannot but share their benefits with one another.

Now, it is very important for us to know what benefit we shall gain from this. The basis on which we believe the church is that we are fully convinced we are members of it. In this way our salvation rests upon sure and firm supports, so that, even if the whole fabric of the world were overthrown, the church could neither totter nor fall. First, it stands by God's election, and cannot waver or fail any more than his eternal providence can. Secondly, it has in a way been joined to the steadfastness of Christ, who will no more allow his believers to be estranged from him than that his members be rent and torn asunder. Besides, we are certain that, while we remain within the bosom of the church, the truth will always abide with us. Finally, we feel that these promises apply to us: "There will be salvation in Zion" [Joel 2:32; Obad. 17]; "God will abide in the midst of Jerusalem forever, that it may never be moved" [Ps. 46:5]. So powerful is participation in the church that it keeps us in the society of God. In the very word "communion" there is a wealth of comfort because, while it is determined that whatever the Lord bestows upon his members and ours belongs to us, our hope is strengthened by all the benefits they receive. . . .

The visible church as mother of believers

But because it is now our intention to discuss the visible church, let us learn even from the simple title "mother" how useful, indeed how necessary, it is that we should know her. For there is no other way to enter into life unless this mother conceive us in her womb, give us birth, nourish us at her breast, and lastly, unless she keep us under her care and guidance until, putting off mortal flesh, we become like the angels [Matt. 22:30]. Our weakness does not allow us to be dismissed from her school until we have been pupils all our lives. Furthermore, away from her bosom one cannot hope for any forgiveness of sins or any salvation, as Isaiah [Isa. 37:32] and Joel [Joel 2:32] testify. Ezekiel agrees with them when he declares that those whom God rejects from heavenly life will not be enrolled among God's people [Ezek. 13:9]. . . . By these words God's fatherly favor and the especial witness of spiritual life are limited to his flock, so that it is always disastrous to leave the church.

Marks and authority of the church

We have laid down as distinguishing marks of the church the preaching of the Word and the observance of the sacraments. These can never exist without bringing forth fruit and prospering by God's blessing. I do not say that wherever the Word is preached there will be immediate fruit; but wherever it is received and has a fixed abode, it shows its effectiveness. However it may be, where the preaching of the gospel is reverently heard and the sacraments are not neglected, there for the time being no deceitful or ambiguous form of the church is seen; and no one is permitted to spurn its authority, flout its warnings, resist its counsels, or make light of its chastisements—much less to desert it and break its unity. For the Lord esteems the communion of his church so highly that he counts as a traitor and apostate from Christianity anyone who arrogantly leaves any Christian society, provided it cherishes the true ministry of Word and sacraments. He so esteems the authority of the church that when it is violated he believes his own diminished.

Institutes IV. 1:1–4, 10

6

The Chief End of Human Life

THE SERVICE OF GOD

[Guillaume Farel, the first Reformer of Geneva and Calvin's friend, had urged Calvin to return to Geneva. In a letter Calvin explains that he is returning against his personal inclinations as an act of obedience to God.]

As to my intended course of proceeding, this is my present feeling: had I the choice at my own disposal, nothing would be less agreeable to me than to follow your advice. But when I remember that I am not my own, I offer up my heart, presented as a sacrifice to the Lord.... And for myself, I protest that I have no other desire than that, setting aside all consideration of me, they may look only to what is most for the glory of God and the advantage of the Church. Although I am not very ingenious, I would not want pretexts by which I might adroitly slip away, so that I should easily excuse myself in the sight of men, and show that it was no fault of mine. I am well aware, however, that it is God with whom I have to do, from whose sight such crafty imaginations cannot be withheld. Therefore I submit my will and my affections, subdued and held-fast, to the obedience of God; and whenever I am at a loss for counsel of my own, I submit myself to those by whom I hope that the Lord himself will speak to me.

Written in 1541

THE GLORY OF GOD

1. *Minister. What is the chief end of human life?*
Child. To know God by whom we were created.
2. *M. Why do you say that?*
C. Because He created us and placed us in this world to be glorified in us. And it is indeed right that our life, of which He Himself is the beginning, should be devoted to His glory.
3. *M. What is the highest good of man?*
C. The same thing.
4. *M. Why do you hold that to be the highest good?*
C. Because without it our condition is more miserable than that of brute-beasts.
5. *M. Hence, then, we see that nothing worse can happen to a man than to live without God.*
C. It is so.
6. *M. What is the true and right knowledge of God?*
C. When we know Him in order that we may honor Him.
7. *M. How do we honor Him aright?*
C. By putting our trust entirely in Him, by serving Him in obedience to His will, by calling upon Him in

all our need, seeking salvation and every good thing in Him, and acknowledging with heart and mouth that all our good proceeds from Him.

The Geneva Catechism, 1542

Sources

Selections from *Calvin: Institutes of the Christian Religion* are taken from The Library of Christian Classics edition, Volumes 20 and 21, edited by John T. McNeill and translated by Ford Lewis Battles. Philadelphia: Westminster Press, 1960. Readers are referred to this edition, which has an elaborate critical apparatus and copious notes and indexes, if they wish to undertake further study of the text.

The prayers are from *Calvin's Tracts*, Volume 2, translated from the original Latin and French by Henry Beveridge. Edinburgh: The Calvin Translation Society, 1851.

The sermon on election is taken from John Calvin's *Sermons on the Epistle to the Ephesians*, a revision of the English translation of Arthur Golding. Carlisle, PA: The Banner of Truth Trust, 1973.

The best reference for the original text of the catechism is the *Opera Selecta, Joannis Calvini*, Volume 2, edited by Peter Barth and Dora Scheuner. West Germany: Chr. Kaiser, 1952.

Calvin's letters can be found in the *Letters of John Calvin*, edited and translated by Jules Bonnet. Philadelphia: Presbyterian Board of Publication, 1858. Cf. *Corpus Reformatorum, Opera Calvini*, Volume 11, column 99–100 for critical reference.

Scripture passages in Calvin's prayers are from the Revised Standard Version of the Bible.